Canadian Biography Series

FARLEY MOWAT: WRITING THE SQUIB

Farley Mowat

WRITING THE SQUIB

John Orange

ECW PRESS

CANADIAN CATALOGUING IN PUBLICATION DATA

Orange, John.
Farley Mowat : writing the squib

(Canadian biography series)
ISBN 1-55022-186-8

1. Mowat, Farley, 1921– – Biography. 2. Authors,
Canadian (English) – 20th century – Biography.   1. Title.

PS8526.O94Z75 1993   C818'.5409   C94-930007-1
PR9199.3.M68Z75 1993

This book has been published with the assistance of the
Ministry of Culture, Recreation and Tourism of the Province
of Ontario, through funds provided by the Ontario
Publishing Centre, and with the assistance of grants from
the Department of Communications, The Canada Council, the
Ontario Arts Council, and the Government of Canada through
the Canadian Studies and Special Projects Directorate of the
Department of the Secretary of State of Canada.

Design and imaging by ECW Type & Art, Oakville, Ontario.
Printed by Imprimerie Gagné, Louiseville, Québec.

Distributed by General Distribution Services,
30 Lesmill Road, Toronto, Ontario M3B 2T6,
(416) 445-3333, (800) 387-0172 (Canada), FAX (416) 445-5967.

Distributed to the trade in the United States exclusively
by InBook, 140 Commerce Street, P.O. Box 120261,
East Haven, Connecticut, U.S.A. 06512,
(203) 467-4257, FAX (203) 469-7697
Customer service: (800) 253-3605 or (800) 243-0138.

Published by ECW PRESS,
1980 Queen Street East,
Toronto, Ontario M4L 1J2.

ACKNOWLEDGEMENTS

I would like to thank Farley and Claire Mowat for their cooperation and hospitality throughout this project, along with Mary Elliott and Terry Mosher (Aislin) for their assistance. King's College also contributed research funds for some of the expenses. Special thanks go to Cynthia Sugars for her advice and aid in seeing the manuscript through to its final form.

PHOTOGRAPHS: Cover photo by Paul Orenstein, 1982, used by permission of the photographer; frontispiece photograph by Fred Phipps © 1988, used by permission of the photographer and CBC Television; illustrations 2 through 13, 15, 16, and 18 are used with the permission of Farley and Claire Mowat; illustration 14 by John de Visser © 1978, used by permission of the photographer; illustration 17 is credited to Ray Webber © 1978; illustration 19 by Terry Mosher ("Aislin") © 1991, used by permission of the artist; illustration 20 used by permission of Farley Mowat.

TABLE OF CONTENTS

LIST OF ILLUSTRATIONS

Farley Mowat

WRITING THE SQUIB

Introduction

Angus Mowat used to say that his son Farley was conceived on a hot August day under the grandstand at the Canadian National Exhibition in Toronto. His wife, Helen, denied it. Angus's reply was that if it weren't true, it ought to be. He would sometimes switch to an alternative anecdote involving a green canoe beside Indian Island on the Bay of Quinte. Helen would deny that one too. The penchant for storytelling in both father and son raises some tricky issues for a Mowat biographer. That story about the grandstand may be factual, but probably is not. The character of Angus does not exclude the possibility completely, however. In any event, it is the tone of the story that is intended to capture its truth, not the accuracy of its factual detail. A biographer has to remain as close as possible to what might be called documentary realism, while at the same time acknowledging that the truth of an event and a personality is largely contained in such things as tone and texture, historical, psychological, and emotional context. Folding one responsibility into the other is hazardous at any time, but particularly when one is dealing with a natural storyteller of what are sometimes, even often, tall tales.

Farley Mowat is fond of a distinction he makes between "facts" and "truth." He has said repeatedly that he believes in the truth of subjective experience over objective data or statistics. In an article for the *Canadian Library Journal* concerning the collection of his papers at McMaster University, Mowat proclaimed: "My battle cry has been: Never Let The Facts Interfere With The Truth." Since over a dozen of his books are heavily autobiographical, Mowat's biographer is faced with the formidable duty of separating the actual from the invented portions of his memories, without distorting what Mowat perceived to be their ring of truth. Both historian and artist, Mowat depends heavily on techniques of hyperbole, ironic understatement, colourful elaboration, entertaining dialogue, and anecdote. Sometimes he creates a fictional character called "Farley Mowat" about whom he can make disparaging jokes; sometimes he develops a public persona who helps him sell books. There is, no doubt, a third, private Farley Mowat, known only to those closest to him, and this one is the complex personality that the reader of a biography may hope to get to know a little better.

Compounding the biographer's problem is Mowat's consistent assertion (who knows how seriously) that he has no conscious memory, only an "unconscious memory" at the back of the brain where he metaphorically locates instinct, the subconscious, feelings, intuition — what he likens, in a 1979 interview with Wayne Grady, to "the old animal within." "Truth" is subjective for Mowat, and apparently the subconscious mind never lies. The writer will "soak in the truth without remembering the details or even reading about it at all," said Mowat when interviewed by Jay Myers in 1977. Under these conditions, the biographer has to worry about the reliability of Mowat's ostensibly autobiographical texts, for, from a biographer's point of view, an accurate memory in an autobiographical account is an invaluable asset. If our subject's memory, though, is closer to the mechanisms that create dreams, then where and how does the biographer draw the line? These are not Mowat's problems, of course, since he has consistently described his writing as "subjective non-fiction" and stuck to his guns in practice.

Any solution to these problems is tied up with two other issues. First, this is a biography of a person who is still very much alive and active, and whose right to privacy must be respected; many of the files in the manuscript collection at

McMaster University are sealed for this reason. There are, no doubt, interesting and relevant episodes in Mowat's life that, for reasons of discretion and good sense, must be left to future biographers. My account has been confined to what he himself has agreed to put on the public record in his writings and interviews. The bulk of the information included here has been compiled from autobiographical works by both Farley and Claire Mowat, as well as from interviews, letters, films, and a lengthy taped interview that Farley Mowat granted to me in the spring of 1992. I have taken care to include events that he has verified for me; in some cases I have been able to cross-reference information among the various works and interviews. Farley Mowat has been extremely generous in answering my questions, in reviewing the accuracy of the manuscript (as far as his memory serves him), and in furnishing information from notes for "Born Naked," an autobiography he has been contemplating for some time and which he began to write in 1992. The Mowats have also kindly let me go through their photo albums for the illustrations in this text.

The second issue is that I am only a recent acquaintance of Farley Mowat and hence cannot present a complex set of impressions of him based on personal experience. I therefore make no attempt to analyze his character or assess his personality as a bolder biographer might do, since that is a luxury, and a danger, usually reserved for studies of people who have long departed this planet. Here and there I indulge in some speculation about the romantic roots underlying Mowat's ideology, but these roots have been noted before and acknowledged by Mowat himself. Other comments about motivation or development are based on obvious psychological and emotional responses to difficult situations, responses very often described or hinted at by Farley Mowat in his own books. For the most part, I rest on the hope that a faithful portrait of this fascinating man will emerge simply from a recounting of what he has lived through and done so far. The "truth" of who he is will have to depend on the subjective experience of the reader who absorbs the events of Mowat's life through the filter of his or her own imagination and experience. Even Farley Mowat would no doubt argue that it can be no other way. What I *can* say is that

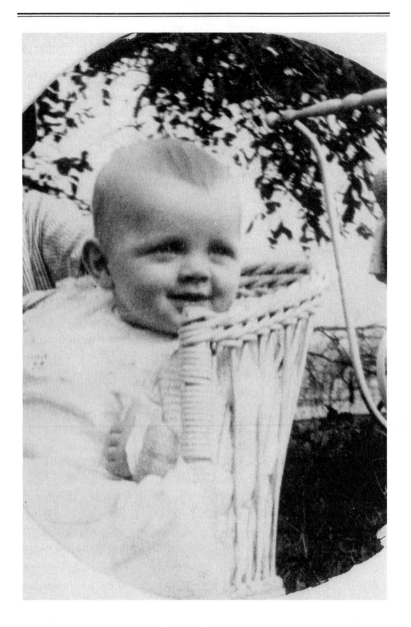

Farley as a baby, 1922.

I have had the pleasure to know two very engaging and stimulating people. My sincere thanks go out to Farley and Claire who have both been very kind and helpful in the production of this text.

Ancestral Roots

The name Mowat is an old and distinguished one in eastern Ontario and can be traced back to Caithness, Scotland, an area Farley Mowat has visited over half a dozen times to walk with the shadows of his ancestors whom he has traced as far back as 1750. The first to settle in the New World was John Mowat, a British army sergeant who came to Upper Canada to fight in the War of 1812. He chose to take a land grant around 1814, and settled in Kingston with his wife Helen Levack. Their eldest son, one of five children, was Oliver Mowat who later became premier of Ontario. Another son, John Bower, born in 1825 and later to become Farley's great-grandfather, was one of the first three students to enter Queen's University. He became a Presbyterian minister after graduating in 1845, proceeded to get his MA, and accepted a ministry at St. Andrew's, Niagara-on-the-Lake, where he was such a success that he was often invited to preach to the local black congregation in their own church. In 1855, he married Janet McGill whose name would be repeated in subsequent generations. She died in December 1856, a few days after the birth of a son, Robert, the father of Angus and grandfather of Farley. Two years later, John Bower Mowat was appointed professor of oriental languages, biblical criticism, and church history at Queen's where he also took on, from time to time, the responsibilities of chaplain, registrar, and chairman. In 1861, he married Emma McDonald, the daughter of John McDonald, a successful Gananoque businessman, and together they had two sons and two daughters. In 1883 he was awarded an honorary DD from the University of Glasgow, an indication of the extent of his reputation. When he died in 1900, John Mowat had lived up to the success and respect that his father had gained in Kingston a generation earlier.

Squib I

Robert Mowat, Farley's grandfather, lived in Trenton with his wife, Mary Jones, and their two children, Angus and Jean. He ran a hardware store that went bankrupt twice before the family told him that they had had enough. Their son, Angus McGill Mowat, was born in 1892 and was just finishing his first year in Engineering at Queen's when World War I began. At the age of twenty-three he joined the Canadian Engineering Corps, later transferring to the Fourth Infantry Battalion, and went overseas as a private soldier sporting the nickname Squib — a name he had acquired in college. A "squib" refers to a fuse made of black powder used to ignite explosives, though the word can also mean a piece of witty writing, a connotation better suited to the next generation of Mowats.

A year later, in 1916, Angus was wounded by machine gun fire and lost most of the use of his right arm. Returning home to recuperate, he decided to revive his courtship of Anne Helen Lillian Thomson, called Helen, a dark-eyed woman with whom he had fallen in love before going to war. She had been more interested in an artillery officer who had since died in the influenza epidemic of 1917–18. Angus's suit stood a better chance this time around. Helen Thomson, whose mother's maiden name, Farley, she later passed on to her son, was the daughter of the manager of Molson's Bank in Trenton, and later Port Arthur. Her family came from around London, Ontario, though Helen's ancestral line stretched back to the Huguenots who arrived in Quebec in the seventeenth century. Together with four brothers and a sister, Helen grew up in a large house in Trenton. She was convent educated (though Anglican), well read, and musical. The dashing Angus finally won her over, and they were married in 1919.

Angus signed on as a fire ranger in the north woods for a short time before moving to Toronto when he was persuaded by his mother to join the grocery business. After about a year working as a clerk for Perkins Wholesale Grocery Stores, Angus grew restless. He was a man who enjoyed independence and who had a name to make for himself, so late in 1920, having bought a Model-T Ford, Angus set himself up as an apiarist on some

*Farley at age 6, with his parents Helen
and Angus, Bay of Quinte, 1927.*

farmland he was allowed to use just outside of Trenton. Although he knew nothing about bees at the time, he was willing to learn; at least he was his own man. But the couple barely made ends meet. Angus used to say that they lived on soda crackers and honey for two years. It was during this period that Farley McGill Mowat was born on 12 May 1921 in Belleville, Ontario — a region that some people have come to regard as the birthplace of English Canadian literature, since for more than 150 years it has provided a setting for writers from Susanna Moodie and Catharine Parr Traill to Archibald Lampman and Margaret Laurence.

Pets and Pranks

Farley Mowat says that his earliest memory is of sitting in the bee-yard watching ants busily crawl around on their hill. In the midst of the ants was an alien bee who seemed to be acting as a traffic cop regulating the movements of the ants. This is an unusually early memory since Farley would have been only two years old, but, actual or not, it establishes the boy's fascination with nature's mechanics. The image also presages his destiny: the presence of an alien who has the power to regulate, or interfere with, the normal behaviour of a highly organized society of ants is a telling hint of the boy who would come to see himself as an outsider in an increasingly mechanized society.

Angus was invited in 1922 to look after the public library in Trenton when the woman who had been managing it retired. He had been and remained a lover of books all his life; Farley thus grew up with many kinds of books all around him. Lean, lithe, and handsome, he was a man no one could ignore. His skills in organization and the energy he brought to whatever interested him, including carpentry and sailing, made him an impressive role model for his young son. Indeed, Angus would become for Farley, as noted in his 1992 memoir of his father, "an overwhelming presence." For father, and later for son, books held promises of unexplored realities, truths to be discovered, dreams to be experienced. They were also a way to make one's name famous, and Angus had his own aspirations of becoming a novelist. He considered the novel the most legitimate form of writing — a bias that would later place no little pressure on his son. For now, though, one can imagine that books were a household preoccupation, and that early on, young Farley realized that one way to impress his father was to read a great deal. He says that he was free to read a wide and eclectic assortment of books as he grew up — including those that were generally forbidden which, of course, made them all the more enticing.

Farley also grew up relatively free of the pressures exerted by orthodox religious or political ideologies. His parents' Anglicanism took them to church from time to time, but no one in the house was overly pious or devout. A healthy scepticism was handed down from father to son, for both came to trust outside authorities only when necessary. Angus was not an official member of any political party, nor did he pay much attention to politics beyond the liberalism traditional in the family heritage. One attitude that was cultivated, however, was a Canadian nationalism defined by traditional anti-American-ism, a willingness to defend king and country, and the ideal of democratic socialism. (In time, Angus would interest himself in the CCF Party, and later the NDP.)

Another example of the formative influence Angus had on his son is recalled by Farley in the film *In Search of Farley Mowat*. When Farley was young, his father used to call him "Plausible Ike" any time Angus thought he was sliding away from forming a distinct idea or evading forming a strong opinion. To Angus, it was crucial that Farley stick to his opinions once formed. From his father, Farley inherited, not only these notions, but also his predilection for wearing a kilt on formal occasions, a distrust of capitalism as a system based on greed, and his love of the sea. Angus was an old-fashioned Romantic, a hold-over from the nineteenth century in many ways, and his son could not help but absorb some portion of his outlook.

Angus loved to cruise around the Bay of Quinte, a bay in the north of Lake Ontario just outside of Belleville, in a dinghy he called *Little Brown Jug*, and then in a somewhat larger vessel he christened *Stout Fellow*. Farley tells a story, which he insists is true, about how, when he was five, his father told him that since he was now a full-fledged sailor and a Mowat, he could have sugar or rum on his porridge. Little Farley chose rum, of course. Another anecdote involves a stay at "Greenhedges," Granny Mowat's house in Oakville (Robert's family had moved there from Trenton), when Angus and Helen went away on vacation. As he has written in *Never Cry Wolf*, Farley found his grandmother to be a frightening woman who "had never forgiven her husband for having been a retail hardware merchant." On a solitary excursion in the vicinity of "Greenhedges," Farley found three small catfish in a nearby pond and took them home as pets. Since there was nowhere to put them, he decided to place them in the toilet until morning. Late that night, when she needed to use the facility, the fish so startled Granny that a cousin who was also staying there rushed to the rescue and flushed them away. Little Farley felt so sorry for the fish, that it set his course for life. It did nothing to discourage his irrepressible collecting of pets, and, he says, probably led in a direct line to his studying of wolves many years later. These are the kind of stories that, even if they are not factual, create the impression of a childhood filled with Dickensian characters and eccentric tension-filled episodes. Whatever the consequences, we know that our young hero developed a keen eye for the hilarious quirks in people, not to mention a feeling that he was different from those in the mainstream.

Because he was smaller in stature than other children his age, Farley had little interest in sports and the other pastimes of his peers. He had been encouraged to be inquisitive and innovative and was undoubtedly very bright, but he learned to enjoy his own company, found solace in his investigations of the world around him, and quickly developed an interest in animals in the woods which seemed close to wherever his family lived. When his father received a better offer from the library in Belleville in 1928, the family moved there from Trenton. Two years later, Angus was appointed chief librarian of the public libraries in Windsor which entailed their moving again. Farley, now nine years old and attending his third school, found that one way to win the acceptance of his schoolmates was to write humorous verses, a tactic that worked well, especially when he wrote a satire about a rather obnoxious fellow student at Victoria School in Windsor. It was at this time that Farley began to collect pets in earnest. He acquired a squirrel named Jitters, a dog named Billy, a cat called Miss Carter, various small rodents and snakes, and a collection of birds' eggs and butterflies. His father also reported that he wrote a letter to the Windsor *Border Cities Star* describing a scheme to cover Canada in sycamore trees because he admired them above all other trees. Weekend excursions to Point Pelee National Park, about thirty miles away, allowed for "field work" in nature lore. Nature had become a major preoccupation for him by this time.

One other childhood character trait that predominates in many of the anecdotes of Farley's childhood is an impish tendency to shock his elders. In *My Father's Son*, Angus reminds Farley of the time in Windsor that he smooth-talked his neighbour, Alex Bradshaw, into lending him enough canvas to make a tent for his homemade circus. Eventually the circus was closed down because Farley had persuaded an eight-year-old to dance nude and her mother found out. He then sold the canvas for a profit. The same source contains a story of how young Farley described to a woman the details of the sex life of the porcupine when she came to the door selling magazines. Anecdotes such as these abound. If the stories are exaggerated, or possibly even fabricated, they do capture the developing personality of the boy, and their "truth" can be tested by reading the humorous works of the mature man. Clearly his sense of humour was iconoclastic, rascally, and often earthy. It would also become a saving grace when his anger or frustration or sense of apartness threatened to overwhelm his reason. Thus Mowat's strategy for gaining attention as a child became a positive attribute in his adult years.

Prairie Pals

The Great Depression was well under way when Angus was invited in 1932 to become the chief librarian for Saskatoon. He prepared for the trip by building a four-wheel caravan, utilizing a space he was offered in the Corbie Distillery at Walkerville, Ontario. In *The Dog Who Wouldn't Be*, there is a description of young Farley working alongside his father, constructing something like Noah's ark on the chassis of an old Model-T pulled from a junkyard. Angus had purchased in Belleville a Model-A Roadster which was duly named "Eardlie" (the family liked to have a name for everything). The Model-A was to pull their trailer-house, complete with a door and windows, four wheels, and a galley kitchen with stove and icebox. In the summer of 1933, they set out across the northern United States and crossed back into Canada, heading west. Chugging through the drought-dusty prairie, the caravan swaying in the shifting winds, they entered Saskatchewan around Estevan and made their way to Saskatoon. If Helen had misgivings about the project at the beginning, she could now begin to worry in earnest: Saskatchewan during the depression would seem like an adventure only to a very imaginative and rugged child.

The Mowats lived in a rented house at 718 Saskatchewan Crescent, then on the north edge of Saskatoon, at that time a city of around thirty thousand people of mixed origins, including Dukhobors, Hutterites, Slavs, Scandinavians, Native peoples, and many of British stock — a cultural mix that must have fired the romantic imagination of the boy. They were only a short streetcar ride from the open prairie, so Farley spent as much time away from the city as he could. His most pressing concern was to get a dog, since in the past he had always had a pet to keep him company in the many new places they moved to — and this was the fourth city Farley had to adjust to in just over eleven years. It is not easy for children to be accepted into new social groups. Farley compensated by making friends with animals, upon whom he projected human qualities. When Mutt, a black-and-white part-setter part-everything-else, was introduced to him, Farley had an instant and much-needed friend. The family acquired the dog from a man named Fuesdale who had bought him from a child selling pups from door to door. Roaming the prairie and marshes with this dog offered Farley enough laughter and adventure for any boy.

Something of the atmosphere of Farley's childhood on the prairies is captured in *The Dog Who Wouldn't Be*, written more than twenty years later. Father and son hunted ducks and geese together with a "bird dog" who was at first more adept at scaring things away than retrieving them. If we are to believe the tall tales in the book, the dog eventually became a retriever to shame all others — and all by dint of his own will and talent rather than through training or coercion. Farley also accompanied his father on numerous trips, visiting people Angus had met while distributing books to remote places. Some of these people were models of independence, ingenuity, and strength — attributes which would have impressed the young Farley, proving to him that "real-life" heroes were not far removed from those in books. As Farley was gradually coming to realize, life, and the way we imagine it, need not be that far apart. He describes himself searching for dinosaur bones, dissecting gophers, camping out overnight with a friend in a poplar bluff studying the habits of a family of owls. Eventually he carried home two baby owls and made pets of them too, naming them Weeps and Wol. They later became the protagonists of Mowat's children's book, *Owls in the Family*.

Perhaps the most amusing episode during their stay in Saskatchewan was one involving Angus's purchase of a sixteen-foot sailing canoe which he insisted on fixing up, remodelling, and christening *Concepcion*. After a few unsuccessful attempts to sail on the Saskatchewan River, Angus joined another land-locked romantic, a Maritimer who had built a boat named *The Coot*, and the two of them devised a plan to sail from Saskatoon to Halifax. The local newspaper announced the journey; gifts and good wishes accompanied their departure. For five days, the boat was sighted only now and again. Mowat tells the story in characteristically farcical fashion in *The Dog Who Wouldn't Be*:

As to what had actually happened during those five days when *The Coot* was lost to view, my father's log tells very little. It contains only such succinct and sometimes inscrutable entries as these: *Sun. 1240 hrs. Sink. Again. Damn. . . . Sun. 2200 hrs. Putty all gone. Try mud. No good. . . . Wed. 1600 hrs. A. shot duck for din., missed, hit cow. . . . Thurs. 2300 hrs. Rud. gone west. Oh Hell! . . . Fri. 1200 hrs. Thank God for Horse.*

The boat sank twelve times in the first six miles. Each time they had to turn it over and drain it. The river dried up in places and the boat had to be hauled over sand and muck until they finally came to water again only to lose the rudder against a ferry cable. After running aground a second time, they were hauled by a horse across sand *and* over water until a downpour finally flooded the river and swept them away at a furious clip, depositing them in a field five miles northwest of Fenton, Saskatchewan, and two miles from the riverbank. Part of the RCMP radio message describing their whereabouts, recorded in *The Dog Who Wouldn't Be*, read: "AGROUND IN CENTER LARGE PASTURE AND ENTIRELY SURROUNDED BY HOLSTEIN COWS. CREW APPEARS ALL WELL. ONE MAN PLAYING BANJO, ONE SUNBATHING, AND DOG CHASING CATTLE."

The family travelled a good deal during their stay in the west. In the summer of 1934, they drove across the Rockies all the way to Rathtrever Beach, near Nanaimo, British Columbia. "Eardlie" was loaded down with *Concepcion* among all the other supplies, while Mutt sat in the rumble seat sporting a pair of driving goggles. This, at least, is the picture Mowat presents in *The Dog Who Wouldn't Be*. Other trips during their stay on the prairies kept them a little closer to home — Emma Lake and various parks and beaches in Saskatchewan.

Farley's first high school, in Saskatoon, was Nutana Collegiate Institute. He had experienced enough trouble with childish jokes about his name at school in Windsor, so when he found himself in a brand new place where no one knew him, he decided to change his name to "Billy." The school was across the river from where they lived, over the Twenty-fifth Street bridge — a three-mile ride on his bicycle. He made friends with children from the Dundurn Indian Reservation as well as at school, eventually persuading a number of them to form a naturalists' club which they named The Beaver Club of Canada. An influential biology teacher named Frank Wilson encouraged such enterprise and in 1935, Farley/Billy obtained an official bird-bander's permit, becoming the youngest person to hold one in Canada. He also took up nature photography after acquiring a Graflex camera, the best in a string of cameras he had tried over the previous years. He took hundreds of pictures of birds

Farley and Mutt in Saskatoon in 1935.

which he learned to process and enlarge himself. Since Mowat took no real interest in sports or other school activities, he found plenty of time to wander the prairie looking for animal life, sometimes alone, sometimes with his father or his friends. Mowat says that he had the usual taste for popular music and movies, but his interest in these things was minimal. Instead, his affinity for free spaces and the natural world grew and intensified.

True North

Early June of 1935 saw the arrival of Mowat's great-uncle (on his mother's side), Frank Farley. He had settled in a homestead in Camrose, Alberta, around 1900, and was now an ornithologist of some note. Frank Farley and another ornithologist, a teacher named Albert Wilk, had come to take Frank's young namesake with them on a fifth expedition to Churchill to study Arctic birds and collect eggs. In those days, eggs were collected and traded all over the world. They left in the first week of June and travelled for three days and two nights in the caboose of the train up through The Pas, where they were met by two more experts from an American university. Then the expedition rode all the way to Churchill, a community on the west coast of Hudson Bay. Near Mile 400, the stunted trees gave way to the barrens, a sight that would stay with Farley for many years to come. At Mile 410 he first saw "La Foule" — the mass migration of the caribou flowing by like a great brown river. It was an image that would so impress itself upon his imagination that for years he would dream of seeing it again; finally it would draw him to the Arctic. For now, Farley was content to spend the next five or six weeks exploring the tundra, finding nests and collecting eggs, learning as much as he could absorb. According to the newspaper announcement of the trip, they were to hire "Eskimo" Harris and "Windy" Smith, barrenlands trappers, who would take them by outboard canoe to Seal River. In his book *Sea of Slaughter*, Mowat recounts how one June morning he was sent to find the nesting site of a hawk. By midafternoon he had located a nest and collected the eggs, with the hawks hovering dangerously overhead. Seeking refuge in a half-sunken and rusting ship, Mowat suddenly found himself confronting three polar bears — a mother and two cubs! The exotic Arctic tapped at his imagination in episodes such as this one — all the ingredients of mystery and adventure, including the captivating Inuit and Chipewyan traditions, called to Farley's romantic soul. He returned to Saskatoon, he says, with a large box of birds' eggs, a tin can containing six live lemming mice, and a crate containing a bird called a jaeger.

Back home, Farley continued to read eclectically from his father's books — from the naturalist stories of Charles Roberts and Ernest Thompson Seton, to more general information on the lives and habits of animals. Farley much preferred to find out as much as he could firsthand by observing animals for long hours, day and night. In early 1936, he persuaded the editor of the Saskatoon *Star Phoenix* to print a weekly column about bird-life in its Saturday supplement for youth called *Prairie Pals*. Mowat's contributions, for which he was paid five dollars a week, were published under the heading "Birds of the Season" and ran from 14 March to 9 May 1936. He wrote as scientifically as possible, and eventually contributed an article on the sex life of the ruddy duck which offended some readers in the newspaper office who pulled the article from the supplement. This is a story Mowat likes to tell, and while it cannot be verified, Angus mentions it in a letter recorded in *My Father's Son*. It could be that it simply became part of the family mythology, whether it happened or not. Mowat and his pals (they called themselves the Beaver Club), with the help of the mimeograph machine in the public library, took to publishing their own little magazine, *Nature Lore*. In one of his letters, Angus remembers how in the first editorial, Farley announced that five cents of each copy bought would go to the betterment of the birds and beasts of Saskatchewan. The practical ecologist can thus be traced back almost to the beginning of Mowat's interest in nature. The summer of 1936 was spent at Emma Lake in northern Saskatchewan, where the sailing canoe, *Concepcion*, came in handy for nature studies until it was time again for school back in the city.

The next winter, Angus was invited to take an appointment as inspector, and eventually director, of public libraries for Ontario. He had been an innovator in the system and had established a reputation for his organizational skills. Helen, who had found the going hard in Saskatchewan, was relieved to be moving closer to their family — there were Mowats (Angus's father, mother, sister and her son) in Oakville, and Helen's parents were near enough to allow her reasonably easy contact. Angus looked forward to being nearer the open water of the Great Lakes and a route to the sea; Conrad was his favourite author, stories of the sea his favourite refuge. Farley and Mutt knew they would find adventure anywhere. The owls, Wol and Weeps, were handed over to a farmer who cared for them for a year until one was accidentally killed in the mesh of its cage, and the other escaped back to Saskatoon where it was shot. Farley had tagged both owls, so he was informed of their fate. Travelling with the Mowats was a young woman who had worked for them in Saskatoon and on whom Farley had developed a crush (he developed crushes rather easily and often from then on). The family spent the summer in their caravan trailer at Lake Kazubazua in the Gatineau Hills of Quebec where Helen's parents had property. There the girl met and eventually married a young Québécois, an event that inspired Farley to write the following poem about the fate of an abandoned lover, recorded in *The Dog Who Wouldn't Be*:

> Still his unseeing, dull and lidless stare
> Earnestly scans the long blue upper air;
> A corpse's gaze — save where a clinging fly
> Scuffs busily across the sunken eye.

Mowat had started writing poetry in Saskatchewan, a hobby he would continue well into his twenties. Yet it seems that his love of fun meant that he could not resist turning this love poem into parody — a temptation he would barely resist when he penned his verses in the next few years.

Farley with coyote, "Fang," in southern Saskatchewan, 1939.

Escape from Toronto

By September the Mowats had moved into a house in Toronto, but after the experience of the wide-open prairies, father and son felt very cramped. The closed feeling and artificial comforts of the large city held no attraction for Farley and continued to repel him for the rest of his life. In *The Dog Who Wouldn't Be*, Mowat describes himself playing in the downtown cemetery just to find some open space — even heavily forested areas, he says, eventually gave him claustrophobia. From early on Mowat was convinced that the unnatural confinement of city life was not the way nature had intended the human species to live.

Toronto meant making new friends all over again at North Toronto Collegiate, though inside of a year, Mowat had made contact with a number of young naturalists through his association with the Royal Ontario Museum. He joined the Toronto Ornithological Field Group and contributed articles to their mimeographed journal, called *The Chat*, which he also edited for a year. School sports and the other preoccupations of his peers still interested Mowat less than the wonders of nature and science. He continued to develop his skills with his Graflex camera and began to practise taxidermy. That summer he decided to go on his first scientific field trip. The idea was to hitchhike to his grandparents' place in Kazubazua, collecting animals and birds along the way to be used as museum specimens. Through his work for the Ontario Museum, he had met a boy his age, Andrew H. Lawrie, who shared his interests, and the two became fast friends on their summer adventure. At this point in 1937, Mowat and Lawrie thought seriously about becoming professional biologists. Lawrie eventually did become a biologist for the Ontario Department of Lands and Forests.

Farley's initiative and skill with the Graflex camera brought him some notoriety with his fellow students. He decided that winter to visit the Casino, a local strip joint on King Street, to sneak some pictures of the current ecdysiasts which he could then sell to the curious. He snapped the pictures as best he could but this drew the attention of the resident bouncers. They grabbed his unwieldy camera, but not before he managed to flip a lever and retrieve the film. The blurred and underexposed picture of an apparently nude stripper did not deter sales in the least, but the experience convinced the young entrepreneur that he should give up any aspirations of becoming a professional photographer. In any event, Farley's parents had decided to move to Elgin Mills, north of the city, a village that felt more like a nineteenth-century museum than a community. They moved into a house vacated by a sculptor, a house Mowat typically describes, in *The Dog Who Wouldn't Be*, as a projection of his own interests and attitudes: "Its front door looked out sedately over the outskirts of a sedate community; but then the house rambled backward through sagging passages until the back door opened on an unconstrained stretch of countryside."

Farley now found himself attending Richmond Hill High School. In that same year, 1938, his father published his first novel, *Then I'll Look Up*, the first of a planned trilogy on the history and cultural life of the area around the Bay of Quinte. The reviews were not encouraging but Angus remained undaunted. There was now established in the household the notion that writing as a profession was both possible and real. The question was: how was Farley to combine a vocation in books with what was amounting to a passionate interest in the untamed lives of animals?

That summer, Farley devised a plan to undertake "an ornithological survey of Saskatchewan," one of the many such great deeds he typically envisioned himself capable of. In the National Film Board's *In Search of Farley Mowat*, his mother quips: "Farley always exaggerated. You know that." She also mentions her surprise when Farley confessed to her his feelings of being an outsider because he was too small for the normal activities of the other children. His love of animals and open spaces was an accommodation to solitude, to the anxiety in all children that they will not be fully accepted. Always a possible compensation is the feeling that nature is a real home, full of animal friends, beckoning adventures, and trials. Yet there is probably more to it than that. Success in the wilds is also a way of making a name for oneself, of establishing an identity not tied to social groups or a particular place, but which gains one social recognition just the same. As he got older, the notion of apprehending the open spaces of the unknown, particularly through a knowledge gained by capturing the freest of animals, the birds, seemed attractive to him. His friend Frank Banfield had a new Dodge, so Farley, Frank, and another friend, Harris Hord, drove to Saskatoon, picked up an earlier friend, Murray Robb, and all four roamed around Emma Lake, then Dundurn and Cypress Hills, shooting and trapping specimens for the museum. Farley even caught a young coyote which he brought back with him to Elgin Mills and kept there for part of the next winter.

Angus, meanwhile, could not wait to get out on the water. One of the first things he did after returning to Ontario was to make arrangements to get a boat. He went to Montreal and bought a large, solid, black, Norwegian-designed *rednings-skoite*, ketch rigged, with a red sail made in Lunenburg. He called her *Scotch Bonnet*, after a black reef called Scotch Bonnet Rock that juts out of Lake Ontario just below Prince Edward County. Angus sailed it by himself from Montreal to Toronto. In the fall, the family took a cruise to the Bay of Quinte sporting Balmoral yachting caps imported from Caithness. The boat was to be their haven in the difficult years following. They travelled all over Lake Ontario exploring islands for wild birds, and enjoying the open spaces.

On 2 September of 1939, Angus announced to Farley that war had broken out in Europe. It was also that fall that Mutt was killed by a speeding car near Elgin Mills. Farley grieved deeply. When he wrote about the sudden incident much later in *The Dog Who Wouldn't Be*, he associated the death of the dog with the outbreak of the war and the end of his childhood: "The pact of timelessness between the two of us was ended, and I went from him into the darkening tunnel of the years." In January of the next year, the family moved again, this time to an old clapboard house on Elizabeth Street in Richmond Hill which Angus christened "Hove To," a nautical expression for a temporary resting place. Since Angus was a military reservist, he was called to service and accepted command of the Headquarters Company of the second, or reserve, battalion of the Hastings and Prince Edward Regiment stationed in Trenton. He had to move there and leave the family at home for a time.

Angus and Farley hoist sails on the
Scotch Bonnet *in Whitby Harbour, 1938.*

Farley took to studying aerial photography in the hope of qualifying for the Royal Canadian Air Force. He did not trust the sea enough to consider the Navy — possibly the prairie influence of the sky again. One had to be nineteen years old to join the air force, so the day after his nineteenth birthday, Farley hurried down to the recruiting station in Toronto to join up. He still looked suspiciously young to the doctors there and was judged to be a few pounds too light. Disappointed, he returned home to reconsider his options. He had already done some writing for the local periodical, the *Richmond Hill Liberal*; in *My Father's Son*, Angus refers to a story about the squirrel, Jitters, and some bird columns that Farley published in this weekly newspaper. Meanwhile, Farley continued falling in love, it seems, and there were birds to study. But then, there was also the war.

Training for Battle

Farley's father suggested that if he really wanted to help his country, he should enlist as a private soldier in the army. For one thing, the entrance physical standards would be less stringent than those of the Air Force. Angus insisted that Farley should follow in his father's footsteps by joining his own regiment, and, since he was too young to be in active service, Farley agreed to sign on with the second (reserve) battalion of the Hastings and Prince Edward Regiment (the "Hasty P's") at Picton, Ontario. The first battalion had been on active service in England since Christmas 1939. Farley, however, was posted first to Baker Company in Picton and later spent the summer and early autumn as a private and batman to lieutenants his age in Trenton; finally he was promoted to Officers' Mess corporal. His company consisted of seventy or eighty part-time soldiers in unconventional categories; they had no weapons, uniforms, or other technological necessities with which to fight a modern war, and they lacked proper training facilities. Farley spent much of his free time aboard *Scotch Bonnet* on short sailing expeditions, and was finally commissioned acting second lieutenant in the militia.

For the first part of the winter of 1941, Mowat pioneered ski-training techniques at Trenton. Towards spring he was placed on the active list and taken on as second lieutenant in the Canadian Army at Fort Frontenac, Kingston. He felt enormous pride the day he led a platoon of properly equipped, uniformed men, marching in pomp and glory to a military band. His father's romantic notions of what a man could be and do for his country were now part of his own vision. The image of the brave, young hero was attractive still, and he was part of his father's regiment after all. At the beginning of May, Farley arrived for officers' training at Brockville; by the end of the summer he was a full lieutenant, seconded to the camp's training staff at Camp Borden. In the meantime, Angus had been posted to District Military Headquarters in Kingston, where Helen and their new dog, Elmer, joined him in a rented cottage.

The fall and following winter were long and Farley was restless. The eager and callow Lieutenant Farley Mowat wanted to be in the thick of the adventure, but was held in Canada doing what seemed to be irrelevant, trivial tasks. He had never had to obey authority so patiently before, or to this extreme, so he was not used to what seemed to him a boring, humourless, rather useless routine. His disgruntled mood manifested itself in a series of practical jokes, confrontations with the authorities, and "getting in the wrong." In *My Father's Son*, Angus tells how Farley and a chum even went so far as to try to get themselves thrown out of the army by disguising themselves as privates and running off to Toronto for a good time. When they were found and questioned, the whole incident was treated as a joke by the brass; the plot failed.

Farley and a few others even tried to organize a Young Officers' Revolt at Camp Borden aimed against the government in Ottawa for refusing to impose overseas conscription. The Liberal government of Mackenzie King had to treat the conscription issue very gingerly for the first part of the war because many people in Quebec, as well as people of other ethnic groups, felt that it was Britain's war and that they should not have to be involved. The government's halfway measures adopted

Farley in the intelligence truck in northern Italy, 1943.

throughout the war to accommodate these people were sore points with the soldiers in battle. In his letters home, Farley often snorted his disgust at the gutless men, whom they later called "Zombies," for refusing to help out. Apparently, even at Camp Borden, Mowat and some others got some financial backing for their organization until they were sent overseas. It was also at Camp Borden that Farley lost his virginity.

Squib II

That July of 1942, the orders came through. The men were taken to St. John, New Brunswick, and put on a ship bound for England. They arrived at a village called Witley, on the edge of the Salisbury Plain, and from there were taken in buses to the First Canadian Infantry Division Reinforcement Unit led by Captain Williams. Mowat's accounts of his war years are fairly extensive. He subsequently published a history of the regiment (*The Regiment*), an autobiographical account (*And No Birds Sang*), and a compilation of letters written from his parents, chiefly his father, together with his replies (*My Father's Son*). Although these works contain the usual exaggerations for the sake of emphasis and some tall tales for self-deprecating humour, nevertheless the three books give a fairly accurate and intense description of just what Farley Mowat, at the age of twenty-one, had to face, and his resulting coming-of-age in a time of terrible upheaval.

Life in England began with the usual interminable drills and long marches, humiliation and exhaustion. It seems as though Mowat was the subject of a good deal of teasing because he looked so young. The gruelling training took its toll on him to the point that he had to be hospitalized for bruised knee cartilages. He convalesced for three weeks that summer by the Thames River and was disappointed to find that when he got back to Witley, many of the others had been posted elsewhere. Yet he was still eager to get into the action. Major Stan Ketcheson, a friend of Angus, gave Farley the name his father had sported many years before — Squib. It was not a name that he welcomed but he cheerfully accepted the joke and even signed some of his letters home "Squib(b)," the extra "b" thrown in to designate "the second." His father sometimes addressed him as "Squib (Mark II)." His mother too had had a nickname for him for many years — Bunje, which Farley says was derived from a character in a novel by H.G. Wells.

Finding a proper place for Lieutenant Mowat while the troops were being trained took some doing. Perhaps those in charge felt he looked too young to get the attention of a rifle company. He had decided to grow a moustache to look older — a source of amusement, apparently, for the men around him for the next two years. In any case, at one point Major Ketcheson decided to send him to London with some secret documents for Canadian Military Headquarters, thus introducing Mowat to the world of military intelligence. In September, he acquired the services of a batman named "Doc" Macdonald, and was sent as an acting intelligence officer to join the Hasty P's, now in the valley of the River Wal in Sussex. He stayed for a time in Battalion Headquarters, which was set up in a vicarage in the hamlet of Waldron. It was a pleasant place to explore during off hours, observing the bird-life of the English countryside. As the title of his memoir *And No Birds Sang* (adapted from Keats's "La Belle Dame Sans Merci") implies, for Mowat, the alternative to the barbarism of war was symbolized by the delicacy, freedom, and beauty of birds. When they were sent on manoeuvres to Loch Fyne in Scotland, all tranquillity ceased for quite some time. For weeks they practised combined operations assaults on an enemy coast, even over Christmas.

In the meantime, Angus was transferred to National Defence Headquarters in Ottawa where he was to devise a way to get books to the troops in Canada. Helen stayed in Kingston. Partly to fill up the long nights in Ottawa, Angus wrote many letters to his son, keeping him informed about political and domestic events at home. In some ways, the distance between them brought father and son closer together during those important years when a son realizes that his father is not only a father, but also a man. Angus knew what war was like and in his own way attempted to communicate his worry and his love for Farley. Back in Sussex, the battalion waited in the cold rain. Farley tinkered with German bombs and weapons, learning how they were made, how to dismantle them, how to recognize them if necessary — all part of his intelligence training. He says in *And No Birds Sang*:

> Fooling with bombs and other bangers became something of an addiction with me that winter. After four months with my Regiment, I was uncomfortably aware that I was still regarded in some quarters more as a mascot than a fighting soldier. Some of my superiors tended to be a shade too kindly, my peers a whit too condescending, and my inferiors a trifle too patronizing. I needed to excel at something martial and reasonably risky and it seemed to me that a flirtation with things that go bang in the night might earn me soldierly merit and the respect of my fellows.

It was most likely during the winter of 1943 that Farley, too, found a way to make the long nights pass. He began to put together notes for a story about his years with Mutt on the Saskatchewan prairie. He sent a couple of chapters home and got a teasing response from his father that he had stolen "the skunk story" from him. Remembering a happier time with his dog would become a useful psychological and emotional defence in the dark months and years to come.

That spring, he was temporarily assigned to act as air liaison in mock battles, which meant that he had to call in air strikes for both sides. Back at Witley he was given command of Five Platoon and they headed north to Darvel, Scotland. A fellow platoon commander named Al Park became a good friend while they reviewed procedures for assault landings and combined operations in preparation for a major attack. The companionship of Park would help Mowat through the next months. In the first weeks of June the company was given a four-days' leave which Farley says in *And No Birds Sang* he spent in the countryside of Scotland watching birds. In *My Father's Son*, however, he accounts for the time by confessing to a love affair with Hughie, a married English corporal in the Women's Auxiliary Air Force, whose husband was in North Africa. He tells his parents that the arrangement was strictly chaste, but that they wrote to each other whenever they could. In any event, on 13 June 1943, he and his company found themselves aboard the

Farley with situation maps leaving Livorno, Italy, in 1945.

transport ship *Derbyshire* leaving from Greenoch, Scotland, to join Montgomery's Eighth Army which was attempting to drive the Germans out of Southern Europe. Aboard ship, he and a fellow prankster were placed under arrest for playing a joke on a brigadier responsible for troop discipline. Since everyone involved was no doubt roaring drunk, the commanding officer of the 48th Highlanders got them out of trouble.

"Operation Husky"

Towards the beginning of July, all the platoon commanders were informed that they were part of "Operation Husky" — an assault against enemy positions on the southwestern tip of Sicily as part of a drive into Italy from the south. Mowat was now no longer an intelligence officer but, for the time being, was to command Five Platoon of Able Company which would be part of the assault wave against the beaches of Pachino. The *Derbyshire* was part of a convoy of seven big troop ships escorted by cruisers, destroyers, and corvettes. At one point, off the coast of Gibraltar, they witnessed the destruction by depth charges of an enemy submarine, and the reality of war came closer. Sirocco winds threatened to postpone the whole operation, but on 10 July, the order to begin the attack was given. Four hundred vessels of various shapes moved against the coast in rough seas.

As Mowat relates the events, many of the men in the landing boats were seasick; more than a few were terrified. His small craft was blown off course very quickly so that he was not sure where they were landing. At dawn, under heavy fire, the unstable landing craft edged onto a sandbar; they had to get into shore from there. Mowat's vivid, and even humorous, depiction of this event occurs in *And No Birds Sang*:

This was the moment toward which all my years of army training had been building. It was *my* moment — and if I seized it with somewhat palsied hands, at least I did my best.

Revolver in hand, Tommy gun slung over my shoulder, web equipment bulging with grenades and ammo, tin hat pulled firmly down around my ears, I sprinted to the edge of the ramp shouting, "Follow me, men!" . . . and leapt off into eight feet of water.

Weighted as I was I went down like a stone, striking the bottom feet-first. So astounded was I by this unexpected descent into the depths that I made no attempt to thrash my way back to the surface. I simply walked straight on until my head emerged. Then I turned with some faint thought of shouting a warning to my men, and was in time to see Sgt.-Major Nuttley go off the end of the ramp with rifle held at arm's length and the fingers of his free hand firmly clutching his nose. He looked like an oddly outfitted little boy jumping into the old swimming hole.

Quickly, farce turned to tragedy when the sergeant-major was killed by a bullet through his throat. Later, the newspaper account of this landing became part of a good-natured joke played on Mowat by Stan Ketcheson when an American reporter came looking for a story. In *My Father's Son*, we learn that Angus was sent a clipping from the *New York Times* which read, in part, "The mascot of an officers' mess nearby is a youthful Captain who rejoices in the name of Bunje William Frank Farley Oliver Angus McGill Mowat. He is generally known as Squib. Squib, who is exceedingly short, . . . earned local renown during the Sicilian invasion. He stepped off a landing craft leading his troops and shouting 'Follow me!' and promptly disappeared, except for a hand clutching a pistol rippling along the surface." Significantly, Mowat's many names were here listed together; sorting them out would take a few more years.

After establishing a beachhead, the troops were ordered to move north, rounding up Italian defenders as they went. In oppressive heat, Mowat and his men marched fifty miles before clambering aboard some tanks which took them to Giarratano where they had to establish a defence perimeter. Mowat's resentment at not getting into the Air Force began to waver the next morning, after they were attacked by German Messerschmidts: one was shot down and another disabled. As they slowly followed the Germans, death became a more common presence. In mid-July their regiment rode into an enemy trap at the town of Grammichele which was defended by two infantry battalions of the elite Hermann Goering Division, backed by tanks and artillery. Mowat describes himself as watching birds when the attack suddenly began. In a couple of hours, however, the Germans were driven back and the troops moved up hills, through valleys, and clambered up the sides of mountains. In a town called Piazza Amerina a photographer took Mowat's picture by a well, and the photo turned up later in the *London Illustrated News*.

One of the most impressive battles in Sicily took place at Valguarnera in mid-July. That battle, and the assault on the key positions on Mount Assoro, enclosed Mowat in the brutality and horror of war — an experience that would get much worse in the days ahead. The only way to move the Germans out of their secure position on the mountain was to scale their perch by night and launch a surprise attack from many sides at dawn. Mowat's company was given the job of scrambling up the side of the mountain, clearing out sentries, and cutting off the road. In these battles the maps were unreliable, radios did not function properly in the mountains, and artillery resistance was strong. Nevertheless, the First Brigade eventually cleared out German positions, killing many men and taking numerous prisoners. Mowat found himself fighting close to the enemy for the first time. He had to fire on a German position which then went silent, count the dead as they inched their way forward, and search for papers on the bodies. He also took part in very risky night reconnaissance, led patrols into villages hiding enemy snipers, and dragged his dead and wounded men back to safer positions. Mowat's narration of the battles in *And No Birds Sang* very effectively captures the terror, suspense, and shock of the experience. He draws vivid and touching pictures of his comrades Alex Campbell, Al Park, Paddy Ryan, A.K. Long, and others, many of whom were killed or reported missing. By 22 July, after one last rocket killed four men in his platoon, the Germans pulled out of Assoro. Mowat, suffering from dysentery by now, was told that he once again had been assigned as an intelligence officer.

Mutiny Within

After a few days in a field hospital set up in a monastery, Mowat went back to the front line at Nissoria where the regiment was being badly mauled. They had suffered more than two hundred casualties, among them his friend, A.K. Long, who was taken prisoner and later declared dead. Finally, they defeated the Germans in Sicily and rested in the village of Grammichele overlooking the plains of Catania. The newly arrived officers made them train, polish buttons, line up for inspections and the like, so that whatever respect the men had for them, and Mowat's trust of bureaucratic authority had always been very thin, was stretched to the limit. On 1 September, they were moved to the Straits of Messina for the invasion of Italy which began two days later. The weather turned wet and cold from then on, and although Italy formally surrendered on 8 September, moving the Germans out of the country took a massive effort on the part of the Allies.

For the next four months, Mowat moved with the regiment into the thick of the fighting. When a land mine exploded under a truck he was directing, killing two men and wounding seven more, Mowat temporarily lost his hearing, but was lucky enough to come away with only bruises. At one point, he and Bruce Richmond rode boldly into the town of Catanzaro, not knowing whether or not it was being defended. They wound up bluffing their way to the Italian general in charge and requisitioning thirty-one carriers for their cause. On another occasion, he and his men got lost in the fog in German territory, at which time a friend he had made in Richmond Hill, Luke Reid, was taken prisoner, while Mowat and his comrade Kennedy barely escaped with their lives. At Ferrazzano, Mowat was shot in the back but was saved by a tin of bully beef in his pack; his mate, Gerry Swayle, killed the Germans who had shot at Mowat from their car. Later, at Ripalimosani, Swayle and seven of his platoon were killed and their bodies left on the road for five days. At Swayle's funeral, an occasion Mowat describes in *And No Birds Sang*, he was given his friend's spectacles: "for the first time since the real war began for me," Mowat writes, "my eyes filled with tears."

The worst was to come. With the help of the Italian resistance fighters on the mountain at Molise, Mowat and the troops moved slowly to the Bernhard Line. Close to the Moro River, the main battle raged for ten days. They took heavy shelling for days until suffering over one hundred and fifty casualties, decimating the platoon. Mowat was a liaison officer during part of this battle and he saw some of the worst of the butchery. During three days in early December, there were eleven separate attacks and counterattacks, the worst of which found Mowat in the thick of the fighting, forcing him to find refuge from the onslaught in a stone hut that already held four German soldiers, three of whom were dead, the fourth dying. Mowat's description of the episode is as strong as anything in *Catch 22*:

The fourth man — dimly seen in that dim place — was sitting upright in a corner of the little unroofed room and his eyes met mine as I struggled to my hands and knees.

In that instant I was so convinced that this was death — that he would shoot me where I knelt — that I did not even try to reach for the carbine slung across my back. I remained transfixed for what seemed an interminable time, then in an unconscious reflex effort I flung myself sideways and rolled to my feet. I was lurching through the doorway when his thin voice reached me.

"Vasser . . . haff . . . you . . . vasser?" . . . .

His left hand was clasping the shattered stump where his right arm had been severed just below the elbow. Dark gore was still gouting between his fingers and spreading in a black pool about his outthrust legs. Most dreadful was a great gash in his side from which protruded a glistening dark mass which must have been his liver. Above this wreckage, his eyes were large and luminous in a young man's face, pallid to the point of translucency.

The two enemies shared Mowat's rum and the German soldier died. According to Mowat's account of the event in *And No Birds Sang*, this happened two days before Christmas. The effect it had on his spirit is caught in this passage. Later, when sent to lead some reinforcements back from San Vito, the

Farley watching wolf den at Smith Bay, Nueltin Lake, 1947.

atmosphere of death and horror made something in him go dead. He met Alex Campbell, now a major, rushing the new men up to the front; on Christmas Day, Al Park was severely wounded and Alex Campbell killed. A "mutiny within," Mowat writes, caused a "withdrawal of sensation." Coupled with the fear all around him, Mowat called this new sensation "The Worm That Never Dies."

By January of 1944, Mowat was close to "burn out." He was ordered to take a job at First Brigade Headquarters as a liaison officer, and eventually was made brigade intelligence officer. The battles at Ortona, San Nicola, and eventually the terrible battle for Monte Cassino, in May, succeeded in driving the Germans to the east side of Italy. Mowat also took part in the late summer assaults on the Gothic Line near Pesaro and Rimini as well as in the chase through the Po Valley. As acting captain (the promotion seemed to be an on-again-off-again affair for a time), Mowat had a variety of jobs: decoding messages, tracking the whereabouts and formations of the German army, keeping battle maps up to date, keeping the official war diary, writing reports on every brigade activity, overseeing security, studying enemy weapons, and questioning prisoners and refugees. His story is outlined in some detail in the letters collected in *My Father's Son*.

Writing as Solace

Sometimes, during the long hours when he was night duty officer, Mowat would jot down stories and poems by the light of a coal-oil lamp, answering the phone and dealing with radio messages as they came in. During the campaign of the previous year, he had been given an Olivetti typewriter by the mayor of a town they had freed. In March of 1944, on leave in Bari, Mowat had the typewriter rebuilt by the Olivetti Company located there. (On the way to Bari, his train was fired on by a wayward submarine just off shore.) That spring, he also met some old Saskatoon friends at a dance: Norm Cramm, Potter Chamney, and Bill Shaw. Many of the experiences of his childhood came back to him in their conversations. Inspired, Mowat returned to writing about Mutt, a project he had given up when the experiences of the war seemed to forbid humour altogether. By April he had drafted the last chapter of a book he called "Dog's Life."

Mowat sent his writing to his father who had now retired from the army and returned to Toronto as inspector of Ontario's public libraries. Angus enthusiastically attempted to get his son's work published, possibly realizing dimly that his own dreams of becoming a novelist were slipping away. He sent chapters of "Dog's Life," along with his own manuscript, to Reg Saunders, his publisher. He also submitted Farley's poems to *Atlantic Monthly* and encouraged his son to write war stories for Canadian magazines. Angus's second novel, *Carrying Place* (he jokingly refers to it as *Carrion Place* in his letters), was published in this year to more favourable reviews than his first one had received. Yet when Farley wrote a rather tepid letter of appreciation, Angus acknowledged the novel's weaknesses. Angus's letters to Farley indicate that he consciously and earnestly tried to keep his son's spirit alive at this time by making him focus on his potential future as a writer, and certainly his efforts helped to sustain his son through the darkest moments of the war. In the meantime, Helen was making her own contribution to Farley's future by putting the $50 her son sent home every month into war bonds for him.

On leave to Naples in the spring of 1944, Farley became reacquainted with a nurse he had first met at a celebration dance just after the campaign in Sicily had ended. His friend, Frank Hammond, had heard that the Fifth General Hospital was close by, so they scrounged a jeep and paid a visit to the Canadian nurses. Farley was attracted to Ellen (Betty) Brown, from Winnipeg, who had worked in Churchill the year before he had gone there with his great-uncle Frank. Their common experiences brought those days clearly back to Farley's memory, and their relationship would last for the next year or so. In May, the Canadians joined the terrible offensive against the Germans at Monte Cassino. By June, the Allies had entered Rome and the invasion of France began. Farley had said that if Rome fell, he would marry Betty, so his pals decided to play a practical joke on him and staged a surprise mock-marriage. Afterwards, the couple travelled around the south of Italy whenever they got the chance. By June, Farley was back with the First Brigade as brigade intelligence officer with an office and staff of his own. He also received a 39/43 Star for his actions in the landing at Sicily. The next month Betty was sent back to England.

July and August were terrible. Mowat suffered from what he called "whiz-bang" nerves, almost chronic diarrhea, a touch of malaria, and was particularly anguished by the incompetence of the commanding staff. His mood was summed up in a letter to his father. It contains an opinion that would only strengthen as Mowat got older:

> Perhaps a hundred years hence the bloodied remnant of humanity will, in its ultimate desperation, find a way to eliminate the twin cancers of greed and war, but I doubt it. It might be amusing to hear what the next dominant animal species on this planet will have to say about us. "Lord, what pitiable fools"? (136)

Even a trip to Rome simply depressed him more: he concluded that cities were places for worms, not human beings.

Mowat had begun writing stories based on his experiences and observations, some of which he sent home to his father. He was reading the books his father sent him — an eclectic selection from Boccaccio to Jerome K. Jerome. In November, he found himself in Naples living in the fine apartment of an Italian widow while he took another course in intelligence work. Mowat wrote to his father that he would never feel at home in Canada again — "Not in the Canada I knew. I have the scary feeling that *it* is gone for good." At the same time he gave up trying to write serious poetry. Apparently, the romanticism of his youth was fading, but it was not dead. His father managed to get *Maclean's* interested in a story called "Stephen Bates," but the army would not let it be published under Mowat's real name. Eventually the editor decided that the story was too bitter and substituted a weaker one called "Liaison Officer," published, in February 1945, under the title "Battle Close-Up"

47

and the pseudonym "Bunje." This was the only good news to brighten another terrible Christmas. The First Division had met a disaster near Ravenna because of a bungle at Command. The year closed no brighter than the previous one.

Feeling more and more reclusive, Farley turned increasingly to animals. In the winter of 1945, he had acquired a menagerie consisting of a linnet, a stuffed oriole, a stuffed ostrich, a stray dog, and a guinea pig named Desdemona. He had decided to give up hunting animals altogether because he now knew exactly what it felt like to be hunted. It goes without saying that in those days he was getting a reputation for being a bit of a character. His penchant for practical jokes had not abated and only added to the Mowat lore that had developed among his peers. When visited by his old Saskatchewan friend from the summer of 1939, Frank Banfield, now in meteorology, Farley combined their talents to hook up an elaborate exploding weather balloon which they detonated one night over the heads of the Germans.

Gathering Intelligence

In March, what was left of the regiment boarded American landing ships at Livorno and headed for Marseilles. From there it was a five-day trip to Belgium with the First Canadian Division stationed at Oostmalle, near Antwerp. Mowat was still, as he put it in a letter home, in a "state of suspended animation. It is unsettling to find you have to *force* yourself to react to things of beauty, of horror, of pleasure, of fear." After a short trip to Scotland to pick up his lost trunk, he wound up in Shoreham, England, to meet with Hughie, the corporal with whom he'd had an affair in 1943 and whose husband was due back from Italy that May: "After a couple of hours, Hughie and I said goodbye in the driveway, while a covey of destroyers steamed by just offshore, and that was it." Those destroyers in the background are the mark of the writer again: whether or not they were really there, they serve as a correlative for the relationship's destruction by war. Back in London, Mowat visited Al Park in the hospital and then met with a number of "Hasties" on leave. Together they drowned whatever sorrow they felt at a place called the KitKat Club.

By April it was back to work. Mowat was posted to Canadian Army Headquarters as technical intelligence officer with the rank of captain, a new job that involved searching for leftover high-tech German weaponry. He made many forays into Germany to collect various bombs and shells for analysis, on one occasion finding himself in the midst of retreating enemy fire. On another mission, described in *My Father's Son*, Mowat helped to liberate a huge distillery with hilarious results. The distillery contained thousands of cases of liquor of all sorts and the allied soldiers had broken open many of them to form a sea of booze. When Mowat saw the aftermath, he speculated that the unconscious men "would have gone up like signal flares if a flame had been applied to any of them. Surely theirs must have been the most monumental drunk in all recorded history." After the surrender of the German forces in Holland, a formality of which Mowat was a part, life was chaotic. As Mowat wrote in a letter home, he did his best to rid himself of his "repressions, suicidal inclinations, homicidal same, inhibitions and rage" — a resolution that led to an episode involving a beautiful café entertainer named Rita who said she was the daughter of a patriotic Dutch officer, but who was probably a "comfort" for whoever was in control. After a few days with her, Mowat contracted a venereal disease which filled him with self-loathing for a time. Mowat was involved in many exceptional activities during these months. He even took command of a captured German E-boat sailing from Den Helder to Amsterdam, and spent some exciting weeks working with the Dutch underground. As he says in *My Father's Son*, there was too much confusion for serious writing, so he took his father's advice and "created a purpose" for himself.

The Dutch underground commanding officer was a colonel named Tyce Michels who was an innovative thinker. One of Michels's ideas was that the British, the Americans, and possibly the Soviets would all be trying to find the secrets of the German weapons program so they could hoard them and have a military advantage over each other, and over the smaller nations. A current theory at that time was that before long there would be a war between the Americans and the Soviets that would draw all other nations into it. Neither Canada nor Holland had any expertise in weapons, so Michels and Mowat devised a plan to round up all the examples of superior German weaponry they could find. In June, Mowat set up a group ostensibly dedicated to collecting weapons and equipment for a war museum in Canada. He had three young lieutenants working for him — Mike Donovan, Jimmy Hood, and Butch Schoone — who, together with Mowat, collected over nine hundred tons of modern German guns of all sorts, a high-speed motor boat, ammunition, tanks, including an MKV Panther, and electronic equipment. When this collection came under the scrutiny of the top brass, they decided to reply by aggressively expanding it. With the help of a Colonel Harrison, who agreed to act as a sort of bureaucratic lookout, they eventually unearthed two V-1 rockets — one a manned model for suicide missions — and a huge tank gun. Donovan and Hood, who were detailed to get a V-2 rocket, apparently got the guards drunk and managed to abscond with one V-2 which Mowat later disguised as a "one-man submarine" complete with a wooden conning tower and propeller. The whole contraption was painted blue.

By the fall of 1945, things were beginning to settle down. Angus suggested to Farley that he had never really needed self-discipline before he enlisted. Yet, with army discipline now discredited in Farley's mind, he would need to develop a new inner discipline, though not until after some rest. The need for constraint is apparent in some of the episodes Farley recounts in letters to his father. At one point Farley was nearly blasted away by a bomb with mistakenly coloured fuse wires with which he had been tinkering; later, he took one of his confiscated mini-tanks on a pub-crawl:

It was conducted sitting on top of a Jerry mini-tank about four feet long which looks as if it was designed as a child's war toy. In fact, it is a battery-driven remote-controlled crawler tractor intended to make its way across no man's land with its belly filled with HE to blow up enemy strong points. Don't know how well it worked in battle but it is a swell device for pub crawls. If you should fall off, you haven't far to fall. Best of all, you never have to dismount. It goes right through the doorways, clanks loudly across the tile floors and comes to a stop so that the driver is at elbow level to the bar.

Despite these escapades, Mowat began to feel that he could again focus on what was important to him. He wrote a short story in just four days. In July, his father had two of Farley's stories accepted by *Saturday Night* magazine and published in the August and September issues. To his father, Mowat wrote of other developments in his life. He befriended a woman from Montana named Helen Miller who loved "horses and Canadians, in that order," and somehow managed to get his collection of armaments past a labyrinthine bureaucracy and aboard the Dutch ship ss *Blommersdyk* bound for Canada late in the fall. On 15 November, the ship and its cargo arrived in Montreal after a rough crossing of the Atlantic.

The staff in Ottawa, where Mowat spent the next five months, could not figure out who was responsible for this mountain of metal, nor what to do with it. For a few weeks Mowat visited his parents, now back in Richmond Hill, before returning to Ottawa to deal with the military fallout. Eventually, he arranged to have the V-2 rocket delivered to Defence Research people in Val Cartier where it was dismantled and studied for the development of high altitude rockets in Canada. This kind of research was later dropped, and almost everything else in the collection was either lost, damaged by fire and water, junked, or sold for scrap. In April, Mowat took his honourable discharge from the army and began to work through the emotional and psychological traumas of the last five years. His idea was to assuage his anger and frustration by getting away from people for awhile. The obvious choice was to return to his childhood refuge of Saskatchewan and to the inhabitants of the air.

Farley at Nueltin Lake in 1948 with the People of the Deer, including Ootek at far left and Ohoto II at far right.

Purging the "Worm"

The summer months of 1946 Farley spent roaming in his jeep through northern Saskatchewan near Lac La Ronge, collecting birds for the Royal Ontario Museum. He quickly lost all interest in killing birds, however. As he puts it in *People of the Deer*: "The search for tranquillity which had led me hopefully into science had failed, for now I could see only a brutal futility in the senseless amassing of little bird mummies which were to be preserved from the ravages of life in dark rows of steel cabinets behind stone walls." Mowat spent a good deal of time in a remote Native settlement, trying to figure out his next step. Reminded by an old man named Henry Moberly of the caribou in the barrens, Mowat filed the image away for the near future, embracing the caribou as his totem spirit when he returned to the city. Although he had given up any plans to be a professional biologist, Mowat found he could not write about the war either. Instead, he decided to act on his father's suggestion and learn some inner discipline by attending university in Toronto. That fall and winter were spent taking courses in whatever seemed interesting — anthropology, zoology, botany, astronomy, literature — for a liberal arts degree. His attendance, he says, was fitful. He took zoology in order to be a "student of the deer" when he next visited the Arctic.

Sometime that winter, Mowat met an army friend whose father owned some old mining reports describing activities in the Canadian north. He knew of Mowat's interest in the Arctic and handed him the papers, one of which was an 1896 publication — *Report on the Dubawnt, Kazan, and Ferguson Rivers and the North West Coast of Hudson Bay* — by Joseph Burr Tyrell who had crossed the Barrenlands of Keewatin from north to south and met a people he called "People of the Deer." This report whetted Mowat's curiosity, and he hunted in vain for more information. A letter from a former RCMP officer who had gone into the barrenlands after a murder suspect also impressed Mowat with its description of the open spaces. So, at the end of the university term, Mowat arranged to go north with a much older American zoologist on a science grant from the Arctic Institute. In May of 1947, equipped with a camera, sleeping bag, and carbine rifle, Mowat boarded a train for Churchill in the hope that in his travels he would meet some of the People of the Deer.

Churchill was a desolate and foreboding place. One day, though, Mowat followed an excited crowd to the pier where he caught sight of a rare bowhead whale, an experience that would later direct his attention to the sea. Coincidentally, Mowat bumped into a man he had met when he was in Churchill as a youngster with his great-uncle Frank. This man put him in touch with a pilot named Johnny Bourasso who owned a twin-engine Anson aircraft. One story led to another until someone mentioned a German immigrant trader who had stayed behind at a trading post with his Cree wife and five children long after the trading had stopped. The camp the family had stayed in, now all but abandoned, was situated at the mouth of Windy River on Nueltin Lake, on the border of lands inhabited by the Ihalmiut, the People of the Deer. Mowat persuaded Bourasso to take them into the camp at Windy River, roughly three hundred miles northwest of Churchill, and in early June, the two men and five hundred pounds of supplies landed near the cabin. While waiting at the abandoned camp, Mowat spent some time studying a family of wolves he found at a place he called Wolf Knoll near Smith Bay on Nueltin Lake; his "Wolf Den Notes," dated 13 June–6 July, are included in his collection of papers at McMaster University.

A week later, still at Nueltin Lake, Mowat and Bourasso met Charles Schroeder, one of the sons of the German trapper and his Cree wife, who had been carrying food to the starving Ihalmiut now camped beside three little lakes some distance away. Mowat was still anxious to meet the Native people of the area and decided to accompany Charles on the journey. In their travels, Mowat learned how the Ihalmiut survived in the harsh, but strangely beautiful, barrenlands. It took a week of paddling and walking, through barrens thick with flies, to cover the sixty miles into Little Lakes. Finally, Mowat saw for the first time what was left of the Ihalmiut: about forty-nine people. Two men, called Ohoto and Ootek, talked to him through Charles, telling of their situation and demonstrating their skills and customs. Mowat, who had developed a romantic view of nature as he was growing up, saw in the Ihalmiut culture a lifestyle consistent with his evolving notion of the pure life lived in the delicate equilibrium that sustains nature, an equilibrium thrown completely out of kilter by the coming of the Europeans — and he had had enough of the European brand of destruction during the war. The more he heard of the conditions of the people, the more enraged he became. In a way, the plight of the People of the Deer paralleled the shattering, during the horrors of the past five years, of his own contented childhood hours spent in nature. The introduction of trapping in order to trade for guns and prepared foodstuffs, along with various government, corporate, and missionary schemes, had conspired to doom traditional Native cultures, thus threatening the very survival of these people. Because the caribou were disappearing, the Native people of the Keewatin area were often starving, and many were vulnerable to disease because of the desperate conditions. Mowat's study of the wolves was taking second place to his concern for the people of the area.

In the middle of the summer, Mowat joined Charles for a six-hundred-mile round-trip by canoe south to Brochet in northern Manitoba in order to procure supplies for himself and the Ihalmiut. At the Brochet post on Reindeer Lake, he met an old, white trader who told him many stories of the Ihalmiut — stories that Mowat wrote down for future use. In the meantime, Charles radioed The Pas asking for help for the People of the Deer, a message that eventually brought government agents in to see them, though not much was done to alleviate the people's suffering. While at Brochet, Mowat learned that the pilot who had brought him in, Johnny Bourasso, was now missing and presumed dead in the barrens. Since Charles could not go back with the supplies to Windy River alone, Mowat made the trip back with him. In late September they travelled for six weeks by canoe from Nueltin Lake all the way to Churchill, and Mowat had many more opportunities to learn the stories of the people he had met over the previous few months. When he returned to Toronto, he wrote a report to the Department of Mines and Resources, the federal agency responsible for the Inuit at the time, informing them of the condition of the Natives of the barrenlands.

Farley, David, Frances, and Sandy at David's
christening near Palgrave, Ontario.

Northern Exposure

The experiences of the summer nagged at Mowat during most of the next winter. That fall he fell in love with a fellow student he had met at the university the previous semester, Frances Thornhill, and they were married in December of 1947. Mowat was anxious to return to the Arctic, so he prepared a plan to study the caribou. He persuaded his old friend, Andrew Lawrie, who had left the navy to study biology, to return with him to Keewatin in the spring of 1948. The federal government took an interest in the project and agreed to employ the two men as student biologists. Apparently, the deputy commissioner of the Northwest Territories told Mowat not to concern himself with the Inuit who, he had been assured, were happy and healthy. In May, the two friends found themselves on a Canadian Forces air transport flying in to Churchill. By coincidence, Mowat met Charles there who gave him the alarming news that the caribou had been so scarce that winter that the Natives could hardly subsist: they had been able to save nothing for the spring and by March were starving again. Charles reported that the supplies sent by the government were still sitting in Churchill, so Mowat arranged to have them loaded aboard the aircraft that took him and Lawrie to the cabin in Windy River.

By early June, they had again made contact with Ootek, Ohoto, Pommela, Owliktuk, and the rest of those who were left of the People of the Deer. On hearing the details of the terrible winter, and after witnessing the present suffering of the people, Mowat and Lawrie used their radio transmitter to request emergency supplies of food and ammunition, but no action was taken by the government. By mid-June the hunger was so acute that they handed over some of their own supplies and radioed again. In reply, they were told not to interfere and to make do as best they could. Mowat, determined to learn what he could of the Ihalmiut language, asked for some lessons, and eventually got to the point where he could make himself understood in a rudimentary fashion. At least he could understand something of the people's stories and get information about the local animals and plants. Throughout, he collected notes on everything he learned. Mowat and Lawrie took the opportunity to travel to the various camps around Nueltin and Angikuni Lakes, all the while realizing that things were getting worse for the Ihalmiut. They left as much of their own provisions as they dared and radioed again that the people were desperate for food. In July, a plane landed with supplies for them, but none for the Ihalmiut. They flew north to study wildlife for a month, assuming that help would arrive, but returning to Windy Cabin in August, they found that nothing had been done. This was a pattern that repeated itself for the next few months.

It was decided that Mowat, now sporting a beard to appear older (a fashion he would sustain from then on), would fly back to Churchill and take action as a private individual. He found the agent in charge of the Inuit in eastern and central Canada and received a promise that the situation would be cleared up. He also visited Lieutenant D.C. Cameron in Churchill and through his good offices was able to gather together some army rifles and ammunition. Mowat had contacted Frances who flew to Churchill, and together they returned to Nueltin Lake. When supplies did arrive in September, they were inadequate; nevertheless, the Ihalmiut responded by arriving at Windy Cabin with gifts. One such visit and exchange is narrated in *The Desperate People*:

> One man might bring a bundle of caribou tongues, while another might bring two or three pairs of finely made deerskin boots. Ohoto, ebullient and irrepressible, undertook a mock courtship of my wife (who had joined us in late August), and on one memorable occasion he sneaked into the cabin during my absence to present her with an immense bouquet of marrowbones. When I selfishly refused to admit him to full cousinship, with all that this implies in Eskimo society, he brought the whole camp to a pitch of near-hysteria with a comic song which he sang to the accompaniment of a skin-drum, and which lampooned at great length the niggardly nature of the small white man called Skibby.

He was still known even to the Ihalmiut by his nickname of Squib or Squibby. Through September and October, until the conditions became too severe for them to remain in this remote place, Mowat and his wife lived close to the Ihalmiut. In late October they took up residence in Brochet for two months while Mowat worked on his wolf and caribou studies. Andrew Lawrie stayed on at Windy Cabin until December and would return the next summer; Mowat learned many of the details of what happened to the Ihalmiut from him.

From Brochet, Mowat wrote to Dudley Cloud at the *Atlantic Monthly* and enclosed a manuscript about wolves. While at university, Mowat had submitted stories to his English professor, Vincent Tovel, who had liked their energetic style and verve. This was an important encouragement for him now to carry on writing. Cloud, however, rejected the wolf piece, suggesting instead that Mowat write a book about the Inuit of the barrenlands. This began Mowat's constructive relationship with an editor who was uncommonly in tune with his writers, a contact which lasted for a number of years. Indeed, Mowat's career as a professional writer began in this settlement on Reindeer Lake. It was when he received the telegram from the federal government with three little words, "You are fired," presumably for paying too much attention to the Inuit and not enough to caribou, that he decided to become a full-time writer. It should be remembered that part of Mowat's decision was rooted in a sense of moral outrage — he saw himself with a mission to teach and reform his own urbanized, mechanized, bureaucratized, desensitized society. Another aspect of this decision was his wish to entertain and attract a large readership which could possibly be mobilized to act. (He had also submitted stories to his English literature professor, who had praised them for their energy and humour and pronounced Mowat a born storyteller, a role he took to readily.) While at Brochet, Mowat drew up an outline for *People of the Deer* which he sent off to Dudley Cloud. The editor's favourable reply encouraged Mowat to return south to write the book.

In the meantime, Mowat had still a few credits to complete for his BA, which he received in the spring of 1949. He also had to find a place for himself and his wife to live. His first choice was to buy land at the head of Lake Superior, but that was too far away from everyone for Frances. Instead, he found some

Claire aboard the Happy Adventure *with
Burgeo in the background, c. 1965.*

abandoned sandy land in Palgrave, Ontario, about one hundred kilometres north of Toronto. He still had the money his mother had invested for him when he was at war — enough to buy ten acres of land and the prefab logs for a log house. Since Angus had always been a skilled carpenter, Farley had learned many building tricks from him. He dug the foundation with a shovel and spent the summer constructing the frame of the house; the rest he figured out for himself. By October they were able to move in and spend the winter on details. Mowat could also take up his writing in earnest, for this was to be his home base for the next eleven years.

Writing for a Living

That autumn Mowat sought the advice of W.O. Mitchell, then editor of *Maclean's*, who told him that if he wanted to eat, he should follow the formula boy-meets-girl-happy-ending in five thousand words. When Mowat sent him a tragic story about the Ihalmiut, it was rejected. Nor did the CBC show any interest. Angus had come across a reference to Littauer and Wilkinson, a literary agency in New York, and on a whim, Mowat sent his story to them. Max Wilkinson quickly sold the story in December to the *Saturday Evening Post*, for much more money ($750) than Mowat would have received for it in Canada. The story, originally titled "Eskimo Spring," appeared in the magazine under the title "The Desperate People" on 29 July 1950. Mowat asked Wilkinson's advice on "slanting" his writing for the market, to which Wilkinson testily replied that he should write what he *must* write and refuse to slant it at all; if it was good writing, he would find a home for it. Later, in a 1953 article for *Saturday Night*, Mowat complained that in a two-year period he submitted seven sad, but uncompromising, short stories to Canadian periodicals, five of which were sent back. When he sent those five to American editors, all were accepted, and he was paid six times as much as he would have been in Canada. Since short stories and articles were paying the bills, Mowat turned out as many as he could while working on *People of the*

Deer. In the next three years he published eighteen stories and articles in such periodicals as *Maclean's, Bluebook, Argosy, Atlantic, Canadian Forum, True Magazine, Saga Magazine,* and *Saturday Night.* Between 1950 and 1955, the majority of these stories were about the people and animals of the Arctic. One of his stories, "Lost in the Barrenlands," published in October 1951 in the *Saturday Evening Post,* was awarded the 1952 President's Medal by the University of Western Ontario for the best Canadian short story of the year.

When not writing, Mowat was getting his property in order: a pond had to be dug, trees planted, the house completed. He also began to get involved in radio work and read six fifteen-minute weekly talks on CBC Radio beginning on 26 March 1950 — a precursor to what he called "Operation Eskimo," his concerted attempt over the next few years to bring the plight of the Inuit to the attention of North Americans. He spent the winter of 1952 finishing his first book, *People of the Deer,* which was published that spring in Boston by Little, Brown/ Atlantic Monthly Press and in Canada by McClelland and Stewart who were the Canadian distributors for the Atlantic Monthly Press. The book was dedicated "To Frances, Ohoto's Friend." Through the Canadian publication of the book, Mowat became close friends with Jack McClelland, a man whom Mowat has told me was "the most important element in [his] career." McClelland was a man of strong beliefs who did not mind, in fact often welcomed, a battle with the established powers in business, church, and government. Mowat's irreverent sense of humour, along with his eagerness to take on the bureaucracy, must have been attractive to McClelland who also liked to light fires under a complacent or silent populace.

People of the Deer was written with a number of purposes in mind: there is passion in its anger and sense of mission; there is also a good deal of artistry in its narrative strategies. The story is made immediate by Mowat's use of a first-person narrative, a vocabulary of emergency and shock, and a willingness to point a finger at negligence and patronizing irresponsibility. Mowat must have realized that it would stir up quite a fuss, though he must also have felt that his name as a writer would become instantly amplified. And that is exactly what happened. His instincts had told him that the truth of a story was to be found in the *spirit* of its narration rather than in the accuracy of its details. While he was criticized in some reviews for errors of fact, and for drawing conclusions too hastily, from the beginning Mowat's intent was to be a "saga-man," telling the stories of Canada's peoples in terms of their pasts and their surroundings. This involved colourful descriptions of places, accounts of personal conflict, and techniques of caricature, melodrama, and suspense. The moralist in him insisted that the general aim of his art be both to educate and reform. Thus he usually presents himself in his stories as in need of education, an approach that allows for his constant hilariously self-deprecating humour.

In *People of the Deer*, however, Mowat had taken on the Hudson's Bay Company, missionaries, and the federal government. He was not to get away lightly. A magazine published by the Hudson's Bay Company, the *Beaver*, ran a long review of the book by Dr. A.E. Porsild, a civil servant in the Department of Resources and Northern Affairs, which attempted to discredit both the book and its author. He listed errors of fact and interpretation, was sceptical about all of the events, and even went so far as to hint that the whole thing was a hoax. The company sent copies of the review to major newspapers and some libraries and refused to print Mowat's reply to Porsild's complaints. Eventually, on 19 January 1954, the debate found its way into the Canadian parliament when the opposition decided to use it to make waves. The minister in charge, Jean Lesage, found himself having to defend policies and practices he knew nothing about; the best he could do was to wave around Porsild's review and, as the last word on the matter, offer to make it available to anyone interested, though he declined to offer Mowat's rejoinder with it. When the book was given the 1954 Anisfield-Wolfe Award in the United States for its contribution to interracial relations, Dr. Porsild wrote the awards committee a letter chiding them for their foolishness since, he said, the "Ihalmiut people never did exist except in Mowat's imagination."

Despite, or perhaps because of, the controversy, the book was a tremendous success. The respected columnist Scott Young

*Farley and Claire at a reindeer farm
in Kolymskaya, Siberia, 1966.*

published a spirited defence in *Saturday Night* of Mowat's handling of the plight of the Ihalmiut. The book was published in Britain, France, and Sweden in 1953; in Germany, Italy, and Norway in 1954; and in Japan, Yugoslavia, the Soviet Union, Romania, Finland, and Poland (often in translation) over the next ten years. This was the beginning of a pattern for Mowat's books, and his work was often serialized in a current magazine or condensed in *Reader's Digest*. The political flap surrounding *The People of the Deer* helped to establish Mowat as a controversial writer, an image that Jack McClelland advised him to exploit. The book also steered him in the direction of popular writing, characteristics of which were compatible with his personality — his merry sense of humour, his impatience with bureaucracy, his championing of underdogs and victims, his taste for rugged adventures in hinterland settings. As the years went by, Mowat constructed a persona by increments, often as situations presented themselves. For now, he was the conscience of a blind southern population, and an imaginative mapmaker of a still unknown land in the tradition of Canadian writing that stretched from Earle Birney, E.J. Pratt, and Frederick Philip Grove, all the way back to Alexander Mackenzie, David Thompson, and Samuel Hearne.

Saga-man

In the fall of 1952, encouraged by his father, Mowat was offered a commission to write the history of the Hastings and Prince Edward Regiment for a fee of $3,000. Angus had been collecting articles on the regiment for most of his adult life. His son still had enough of his father's respect for military allegiance, despite his war experiences (he also no doubt wanted to impress his father), that he accepted the job. That autumn and the next winter, Mowat gathered material; in the spring, he and Frances went overseas so that he could complete the picture. They visited military archives in England, battlefields in France and Italy, and generally soaked themselves in the atmosphere. Back in Palgrave, he completed the research, wrote more articles and short stories, and continued to put the property in order in his off-hours. The book was completed sometime in the late winter of 1954.

Robert Alexander (Sandy) Mowat was born in April 1954, at Orangeville, Ontario. When the household had settled down to reasonable order again in June, Farley accompanied his father and a friend, Murray Biloki, on the *Scotch Bonnet* from Montreal to Halifax. The bird and sea-life that surrounded them on that trip convinced Mowat that he wanted to return to the Maritimes. In *Sea of Slaughter* Mowat tells of passing through Canso Strait, which at that time was being filled in to form a causeway linking Cape Breton Island to the Nova Scotia mainland. There remained a one-hundred-foot wide opening through which the water rushed forcefully; nevertheless, many harbour porpoises played up and down the cataract, keeping the flabbergasted Mowats amused for some time. They were subsequently blown through Canso Strait to Sable Island by the tail of a hurricane. Later, they watched lobsters being caught in Prince Edward Island and saw pods of killer whales in the gulf.

During a storm, the group tied up against a tugboat belonging to the Foundation Company and were entertained by the hospitality of the men who worked on board. The stories these sailors told of salvaging operations fascinated Mowat. When he later mentioned his interest in the lives of these men to his Aunt Frances Thomson who worked for the company, she relayed the information to her boss who contacted Mowat and Jack McClelland. Negotiations in 1955 resulted in an exciting series of books and articles on the daring voyages of the ships *Foundation Frances*, *Foundation Josephine II*, *Foundation Franklin*, all salvage ships that rescued vessels in distress down the eastern seaboard in the 1930s and '40s. The Foundation Company was very open to Mowat's research: they allowed him to examine records, interview employees, and take trips aboard their vessels. They even provided him with their clippings and notes, and made no demands to see the finished manuscript.

Back in Palgrave that year, Mowat also began a long and insistent pro-Canada campaign during which he continually warned Canadians against being swallowed up, economically and culturally, by the United States. He even tried briefly to form a Canadian Independence Committee with Arnold Warren, but hardly anyone paid attention. The year of the publication of the strongly patriotic and nationalistic *The Regiment*, 1955, marked Mowat's active engagement in politics. On the local level, he organized his fellow rate-payers to unseat the municipal government; on the national level, he joined Tommy Douglas in antinuclear peace marches. This formally marked him as a Canadian leftist, at that time a group looked upon by the majority as a small and suspicious association of radicals.

As a diversion, Mowat wrote his first novel for children, *Lost in the Barrens*, which was published the next year and won the 1956 Governor General's Award for Juvenile Literature. The story's hero has a number of things in common with its author. Jamie Macnair, nephew of Angus, grows up in Toronto but joins his uncle in the barrenlands of northern Manitoba because he feels he never had a real home. He befriends a Cree boy his own age named Awasin who becomes a complementary alter-ego. The two get lost for months in the barrenlands, the area Mowat knew best. The book then becomes an adventure of survival, coupling Jamie's clever innovation with Awasin's traditional knowledge. The boys learn to trust each other and, most importantly, always to "travel *with* the forces of the land — and never fight against them." They hunt caribou, run rapids, build a shelter, discover a Viking grave, and survive terrible storms, until meeting up with another boy, Peetyuk, part Inuit and part white (a fictional descendent of the trapper-trader at Nueltin Lake), who takes them to meet his people before going with them to live in the south. The story has a quick pace, brisk, clear prose, and a moral — that the survival of all depends on different races and cultures sharing their best attributes. It reads as though Mowat had divided himself in two in creating the two heroes and indicates how he himself had learned to live a life of divided interests. The book was dedicated to "Jack Mowat who is a real Indian already," as well as to Farley's son and to Murray Biloki. Jack Mowat was an Ojibwa boy whom Angus and Helen had adopted at the age of five in 1951 when they lived in Richmond Hill; they also adopted a six-year-old Mohawk girl, Mary, in 1953. Both children had been living in orphanages before then, and Helen was glad to have someone

Farley swimming with his dog Albert
near Carrying Place, Ontario.

to care for when Angus was away — which he often was from about 1957 on.

The money Farley was now making from book sales allowed him to expand the Palgrave property and add buildings. He was being invited to talk in a variety of places and between 1955 and 1958, requests for articles of opinion seemed to outnumber his short stories. But it was in the winter of 1956 that he decided to go back to work on the stories of his youth with Mutt, the stories that had kept him company during the worst of his war experiences. The manuscript was extensively revised, a good deal was rewritten and added, until finally he had completed *The Dog Who Wouldn't Be* in the winter of 1956.

In 1957, there was yet more research to be done for *Grey Seas Under*, the first of Mowat's Foundation Ships books. Trips to Montreal and Halifax to interview people associated with the salvage operations kept Mowat busy; he also went to sea in tugs to live the experiences of the men. In July he decided to visit Newfoundland for the first time, and at Port-aux-Basques, boarded a coastal steamer and explored the south coast for a few weeks. Mowat admired the ruggedness of the land and the straightforwardness of its people. Besides, the wide expanses of the sea were attracting him as they had attracted his father. After a short time on the French island of St. Pierre, Mowat wound up back in St. John's where he met Harold Horwood who was working for the newspaper there. Horwood was a kindred spirit, a writer with the same interests and in many ways the same vision as Mowat. A rough and ready friendship grew up immediately. It was at this time that Mowat's great love for Newfoundland began; it would preoccupy him for many years to come. Back home in Palgrave for the autumn and winter, he finished writing his first book on the tugs, began work on an edition of Samuel Hearne's journals, and shared in the excitement of adopting another son, David Peter, who joined the family that year. *The Dog Who Wouldn't Be* was published in the fall in Canada and the United States and was an instant success. Mowat finally found himself making enough money from his books that he could scale back on the writing of short stories and articles and concentrate on longer works.

Mythologizing the Past

The Dog Who Wouldn't Be has turned out to be one of Mowat's most enduring and endearing books. The dog, Mutt, is a projection of many of the personality traits that Mowat nurtures in himself: independence; initiative; stubbornness; heroic survival in the face of overwhelming odds, often when everyone has given up hope in him; a penchant for falling victim to accident and circumstance. One wonders, for example, just whom is being described in the following passage: "It will be clear by now that Mutt was not an easy dog to live with. Yet the intransigence which made it so difficult to cope with him made it even more difficult — and at times well-nigh impossible — for him to cope with the world in general. His stubbornness marked him out for a tragicomic role throughout his life." The satirical portraits of baffling adults (represented by the father in the story), the closeness of a boy to his misunderstood dog (with all the psychological underpinnings that implies), the coming-of-age theme that parallels the shambles of the depression giving way to the horror of World War II (Mowat set the time frame back to 1929–35), all conspire to give the story its shape and ensure its appeal to all ages. When the narrator and his dog are forced back to the city, they can only find a parody of lost freedom and nature by playing in the cemetery. When Mutt is killed by a truck in the final chapter (an event that suggests the bogeyman of industrial technology that Mowat grew to distrust in the war), it is the end, not only of an individual's childhood, but also of the innocence of a nation and an era: "The pact of timelessness between the two of us was ended, and I went from him into the darkening tunnel of the years."

The book established another side to Mowat, the writer: his ironic wit, his ability to create farcical scenes, and his vivid memory contrasted with the tone of moral outrage, urgency, and military pride of the earlier books. *The Dog Who Wouldn't Be* is still being reprinted in numerous editions throughout the world. The Seal Books edition of 1980 sold 114,700 copies in the next ten years. The Japanese edition, to choose another example, sold more than 503,700 between 1976 and 1983. The book is still available in at least ten languages, including a

Bulgarian edition published as recently as 1989. It has also been placed on reading lists for school children, and has been the subject of a critical study in the Canadian Fiction Studies series of ECW Press.

Two more books were published the next year, *Coppermine Journey* in the spring of 1958, and *Grey Seas Under* in the fall. The latter is a fast-paced and intense series of stories, told in colourful documentary style, about daring and dangerous rescues at sea. The motif that structures the vision behind the stories is that of the strength and courage of the small (men and tugs) to overcome, if only temporarily, the huge forces of sea, rock, wind, and man's technology turned against him. The forces that dominate this world are, as is so often the case in Mowat's stories, accident and fate. Angus should have recognized the influences of his favourite authors, Hardy and Conrad, in his son's writing. Apparently he did not, for he still wanted to see his son become a "serious" novelist, producing fiction in the classical mould.

The summer of 1958 found Mowat again exploring Newfoundland for six weeks with Harold Horwood. They drove around between Stephenville and St. John's and then went to the outport village of Ferryland. At Stephenville Horwood and Mowat learned from American servicemen and their wives that the United States Strategic Air Command really was storing hydrogen fusion bombs on Canadian soil, and that armed bombers were flying across Canadian air space, even though both stories were continually denied by the governments of both countries. As Mowat tells the story, he and Horwood decided one rainy and bleary night to get the guards drunk and to dump the hydrogen bombs in the deepest part of Red Indian Lake. When he mentioned the bombs on a TV program that fall, John Diefenbaker, then Prime Minister, again denied that there were any such weapons in Canada. This was one remark that would later come back to pester Mowat at the most unexpected time. In the meantime, his attraction to Newfoundland was deepening.

That fall, as a guest of the Hudson's Bay Company, Mowat flew to the Arctic once again in connection with a book on the barrenlands, and again he was pulled into the tragedies of the

*Claire helps Farley get into formal
dress at home in Port Hope.*

Inuit people. He heard the story of Kikik, an Inuit woman who had killed her half-brother to avenge the death of her husband and most likely to save her own life and the lives of her children. She had made her way, starving, through appalling weather, but was finally forced to leave two of her children in a shelter in the snow. One died, and she was put on trial at the North Rankin Nickel Mine for the murders of the two people. Eventually she was acquitted, but not before she was subjected to humiliation and deprivation. At Eskimo Point, Mowat heard more stories of the People of the Deer from Ohoto and the few who were left. The condition of the Inuit was so terrible that Mowat thought at the time that their only hope lay in assimilation with the white culture. He wrote as much in an article for *Maclean's* in 1959. In any event, he left Eskimo Point and Baker Lake with the intention of writing a sequel to *People of the Deer*. That fall and through the winter of 1959, he wrote an outline for what was to become *The Desperate People*.

By this time, the Mowats' marriage was finished. Mowat realized that his way of life and Frances's were not compatible enough for them to stay together, especially as he was spending more and more time away from Palgrave, much of it with Jack McClelland in Toronto. Mowat's thoughts turned increasingly to Newfoundland. That summer he visited the east coast where he studied wildlife and saw *The Desperate People* through the press. Published in the fall of 1959, the book was essentially a clarification and updating of *The People of the Deer*, in which Mowat corrected errors, justified assertions, added real names and places, pointed out that the condition of the Inuit was even worse than previously described, and pleaded that they be seen as a special group of people who could not be interfered with casually, that what happens to their land happens to them and vice versa. Even his own hope that they could be successfully assimilated is judged, in his revised edition of *The Desperate People*, to be a mistake: "For I was wrong . . . dead wrong!" The book, which in the Seal paperback edition sold nearly 75,000 copies between 1980 and 1992, was an enormous success. Like the others, it has been published in at least six different languages. *The Desperate People* was the climax of what Mowat had designated "Operation Eskimo."

Increasingly, Mowat was seeing the problem the Inuit faced as part of a larger picture — the ecological destruction of the planet. At the same time, his interest in Arctic explorers, his kindred spirits, naturally broadened. He began to compile and edit the journals and diaries of the men who had fought the ice and cold in polar explorations. *Ordeal by Ice* became the first volume of *The Top of the World Trilogy*, an anthology of carefully chosen and edited narratives of the endurance, courage, and stubbornness that informed Frobisher's and Henry Hudson's expeditions.

Angus retired from library work around this time. No longer would he pass the statue of Oliver Mowat, his great-uncle, on the grounds of Queen's Park on his way into work. He had succeeded in reorganizing the Ontario library system and drawing into that line of work more men than it had ever had before, including his son's close wartime friends, Doug Reid and Mike Donovan. After his retirement, Angus and Helen moved out of Richmond Hill and settled in Port Hope on the shore of Lake Ontario, closer to the water that would enable further adventures on his boat. Yet Angus continued to be active in setting up library systems for Native peoples and travelling throughout the province as a consultant.

Newfoundland Sojourn

Sometime during the winter of 1960, Mowat and McClelland decided to buy a small Newfoundland schooner together. In May, Mowat flew to St. John's to meet with his friend Harold Horwood who took him to Admiral's Cove where Mowat spent $1,000 on a converted jackboat which became known as *Happy Adventure*. He returned to Toronto with the good news and waited for the boat to be fixed. A massive 1920s seven-horsepower, single-cylinder engine, which did not really suit the boat and required something like a Tibetan ritual to start it, was installed. In June, Mowat drove to Newfoundland and, after another month's work on the craft, wired Jack McClelland to join him for a voyage along the southern coast of Newfoundland in a boat that could hardly stay afloat for a full day. McClelland and Mowat sailed together, in a manner of speaking, to Burin Harbour until McClelland was called back to Toronto. Mowat was then joined by his friend Mike Donovan, another neophyte sailor, with the same nearly disastrous results.

The nautical adventures of that summer are narrated with great zest in *The Boat Who Wouldn't Float*. One farcical episode seemed to follow another, almost always accompanied by alcohol, fog, a leaky hull, and defective water pumps. It was probably on this trip that Mowat found himself swimming with porpoises as described in *Sea of Slaughter*. It was in late July at St. Pierre, when the *Happy Adventure* was in for one of its many repairs, that Mowat first met Claire Wheeler, a beautiful twenty-seven-year-old graphic designer, taking a summer course in French. As Claire describes their meeting in *Pomp and Circumstances*, she was sketching the scenery when she noticed a man "dressed in the most raggedy old pants imaginable and a shirt that was filthy dirty as well as dotted with green paint." Somehow Claire was persuaded to join the crew, and the relationship between her and Farley deepened. She liked travelling and exploring rugged northern areas with him, appreciated his sense of humour, and admired his passion for what was important to him. For his part, it sounds as though he was smitten from the beginning, as he was wont to be. Sadly, when the hurricane season set in, *Happy Adventure* was moored at St. Pierre where, that winter, just after *Ordeal by Ice* was published, ice entered the harbour and sank the boat.

Sometime that year, Lional McGowan of the Foundation Company contacted Mowat with a proposal for another book on salvage operations. Mowat agreed to write about the *Leicester* and the *Foundation Josephine* and made two trips to Halifax to compile information. Once again, the company was very helpful in giving him access to records, a good expense account, and the freedom to write whatever he wanted. The winter of 1961 was spent writing the book and looking forward to the summer at sea with Claire. He also found the time to join a Fair Play for Cuba Committee that February — a publicly reported event that would again draw him to the attention of the United States security services. Along with the Foundation Company book, *The Serpent's Coil*, he put together a small book for children about his other prairie childhood pets, the owls Wol and Weeps, which became the central characters of *Owls in the Family*. Both books were published that fall.

In June of 1961, Mowat went back to St. Pierre to refloat *Happy Adventure* (rechristened *Itchatchozale Alai* and called "Itchy" for a variety of reasons), but the boat was a mess. Eventually he got it running again and was joined at Hermitage Bay by Harold Horwood for a cruise along the south shore to Pushthrough and Bay d'Espoire where they got into trouble and were aided by Captain Ro Penney, the skipper of a steamer called *The Burgeo* whom Mowat and Horwood got to know well before he drowned trying to save a herring seiner in Cabot Strait in 1970. In July, Claire joined Mowat. In *A Whale for the Killing*, Mowat writes that it was this summer that he saw some pothead whales swim into the harbour at St. Pierre, chased there by killer whales. The next day he saw people in power launches chasing the whales, shooting them with guns and lances for sport until they were beached and killed for nothing. As Mowat's concern for the whales intensified, his disappointment in humans was sinking ever deeper.

That fall Mowat left his boat in Milltown and joined his father for a cruise aboard the ss *Baccalieu* along the south coast of Newfoundland. He had left Palgrave for good since there was no longer any point in trying to revive his marriage with Frances. While he remained friends with her and kept as close to his sons as he could, it was clear that he would have to go his own way. From Newfoundland Mowat left for England where he rented a shepherd's cottage for the winter at Coombe Farm near Lytton-Cheyney in Dorset. Claire joined him there in January for what was to be a time of reorientation for them both.

Mowat took this opportunity to research a book that he had been planning on Norse voyages and Newfoundland. He and Claire visited the Channel Islands, toured England and Wales, and wandered through ancestral Mowat country in Caithness, Scotland — the first of many trips there in the next few years. He also got a lesson on the capture and slaughter of whales from a captain of a whaling ship in Thurso harbour in northern

Scotland. By May they were back in a family cottage near Brighton, Ontario, where Mowat completed another adventure book for children called *The Black Joke*, published that fall. He had heard many stories about bootlegging around Newfoundland, especially at St. Pierre and Miquelon, so he decided to compile them into this novel, a task that helped him keep his direction at this confusing period of his life. The story once again involves two boys: one fair and enthusiastic, often to the point of recklessness, and his cousin, a dark, half-Micmac youth, cautious and strong. There is a nationalistic allegory built into the story, though basically the plot involves a number of dangerous adventures at sea which lead to the rescuing of a family boat from an American pirate.

When the weather would permit it again, Mowat was back at sea with Claire in his recalcitrant boat. They had driven to Newfoundland in June and taken *Happy Adventure* on a tour of the coast. They even considered the possibility of staying the winter on the southwest coast in an outport village as they drifted west, but were forced to put in at Burgeo for repairs, ninety miles east of Port-aux-Basques. The village faced mostly rough water, low islands, and reefs, but one could watch seals and whales offshore. The rugged scenery included granite hills, treeless except for some stands of spruce and larch in the gorges; it was the kind of wild beauty they both liked. The friendliness of the people was a welcome sign. When they mentioned that they were looking for a place to stay, they were taken to Messers Cove on the west side where fourteen families lived in a snug harbour. The cost of living would be low, there were no cars, and since they disliked crowds, this proved a perfect retreat. Mowat and Claire bought a five-room, white clapboard house, about six years old, with a large kitchen, a small parlour, two bedrooms without doors, and a tiny bathroom with no fixtures or running water. They would need an office space, and some furniture to be chosen from a mail-order catalogue. According to Mowat's account in *The Boat Who Wouldn't Float*, while renovations on the house were under way, Claire went ahead to Burgeo and Jack McClelland flew in to help Mowat coax the boat there. After they returned in November from the Toronto launching of *The Black Joke* (and receiving the Boys' Clubs of

*The Mowats are "received" by the Schreyers and Prince
Henrik and Queen Margrethe in Copenhagen in 1981.*

America Junior Book Award for *Owls in the Family* — one of many such awards Mowat was receiving from appreciative clubs of all sorts), the house was suitable for moving in.

Outport People

As Claire describes their lives in her fictional memoir *The Outport People*, their house was linked to the houses of the approximately nine hundred people in the community by winding pathways and bumpy trails. There were two churches, Anglican and United, a fish plant whose owner lived in the community, an RCMP constable's office, a post office about a mile away, and a general store operated by Simeon Spencer who was their closest neighbour and friend. Liquor had to be ordered by mail from the Newfoundland Liquor Commission in St. John's and took about three weeks to arrive; if the liquor board did not have what was ordered, clerks substituted bottles at random. There were movies shown twice a week in the old Orange Lodge, and the radio was the only connection to the outside world. The local people never quite relaxed when the Mowats were in their houses, but they frequently visited the Mowats anyway, even if they said little or nothing while they were there. One of the differences that set the Mowats apart was that Farley worked during the winter when the rest of the community was resting or attending weddings and festivals. The Mowats also ate their main meal at seven in the evening while the outport people ate their big meal at noon. The people of Burgeo never understood how the outsiders could eat so slowly, either. Mowat, however, felt he was finally close to people with whom he had a good deal in common. Perhaps he tended to romanticize them as somehow more genuine and "natural" in the Rousseauian sense of nature uncorrupted by the ways of modern social and technological organization.

Whether or not they were fully accepted by the Burgeo residents is a matter of speculation, since any outsider to the community was viewed with some suspicion. One thing that is clear, however, is that the Mowats were easy to get along with, concerned for the well-being of anyone they perceived as needing help. They helped friends fill out income tax forms, got books for the library, organized petitions to the provincial government. As time went on, they inevitably got involved in community concerns. The winter of 1963 saw a campaign for a spring election; the issues in Burgeo — and this gives a sense of just how isolated the community was — were a highway to connect them to the rest of the province and a television transmitter to link them to the rest of the country. When the workers at the fish plant were refused a union, however, the Mowats tried, unsuccessfully, to keep a certain distance from the dispute for the next two years. Telephones also came to the community, which helped the Mowats in their work even though they were on a rather busy party line. Claire Mowat describes the change in behaviour telephones brought to the Burgeo citizens in *The Outport People*:

> Garland and Manuel were not the only two fishermen who made a habit of phoning each other before dawn [and waking up everyone on the line]. It was a curious thing that men who would not ordinarily have dreamed of disturbing other people in the middle of the night now phoned each other at all hours with total indifference towards the sleeping habits of other families.
>
> The new technology cancelled the old rules. During the daytime the same children who had so often sat in my kitchen in solemn silence now took to phoning each other all day long, dialling wrong numbers, laughing, whispering, shouting, and often just breathing into the receiver to sustain the link.

In the midst of this, Farley spent the winter writing *Never Cry Wolf* which Claire then typed (twice) for clean copy. By now a pattern had been established which would be followed fairly consistently for the rest of Mowat's career. He would write his books in the winter and see them through the press in the summer for fall publication and promotion. The spring and summer would be spent investigating new projects and collecting ideas and research for the next winter's writing. A year or so after a book's publication in Canada and the United States, it would be published in England. In the next few years it would be translated and published in many countries. Paperback editions would then follow in a bewildering array so that many of Mowat's books stay in print for extended periods of time; most of them are still available in bookstores.

In 1963 the Mowats were offered a trip to Boston because Mowat wanted to do some research on Vikings at the Harvard University library and at the Dartmouth library in nearby New Hampshire. They were to travel on a new ship that the fish plant owner had bought, but ice delayed its arrival. Since arrangements had already been made, they had to set out on *The Bosco*, an old wooden vessel which took them through spectacular and dangerous ice floes to Gloucester where they were met by Farley's editor at Atlantic Books, Peter Davison. Claire had the sensation that their taxi was racing along roads past trees startling in size. Six months in Burgeo had altered their perception of space and time. From the United States, they visited family in Ontario before going back to Burgeo fog in June. That summer was spent travelling to places in Newfoundland that were important for the book on the Vikings — St. Anthony, Quirpon, and L'Anse-aux-Meadows. They also added a black Newfoundland water dog named Albert to the family.

That fall *Never Cry Wolf* was published to a very enthusiastic reception, except for the usual complaints from academic reviewers who were always sceptical of Mowat's details and theories. Douglas Pimlott, an expert on wolves, complained in *Canadian Audubon* that the book was fiction presented as fact, and that it misrepresented the attitudes then prevalent in the Dominion Wildlife Service which were based on the earlier studies of Adolph Murie and Lois Crisler, works that had already made Mowat's points. Pimlott and others, however, were probably making too much of the scientific claims of the narrative. As Thomas Dunlap points out in his book *Saving America's Wildlife*, the story is essentially a moral tale based on a spiritual experience. The scientist-narrator learns in the course of his study that he has somehow excluded himself from a balanced and ordered world similar to that to which the wolves belong. When he overcomes the impulse to kill the wolves in the den he tries to enter, he experiences shame at his place in the natural order. Once again, says Dunlap, the enemy is "an impersonal administrative program sowing the land with poison. . . . Mowat is overwhelmed by a sense of his own failure to reach the moral level of the wolves and to enter their world. Beneath that is anger and contempt for those who destroy nature." The story is designed to make fun of the narrator's mistaken assumptions; the humour emphasizes the folly of mankind's presumption of superiority. Mowat's concerted attack on a very Canadian reliance on bureaucratic solutions has gone unnoticed too long in the study of our literature. The popularity of his writing could well be rooted in the anxiety and frustration that we all feel when faced with an overwhelmingly amorphous and anaesthetizing bureaucracy, whether its source is government, business, or religion. The book went on to be an amazing international success: at least fifteen translations, in multiple editions, are available to date. The fact that *Never Cry Wolf* has sold millions of copies suggests that its appeal rests on much more than its scientific value.

Happy Adventure was now kept in a slip built for it at Burgeo. Over the next four summers, the Mowats spent a great deal of time leisurely exploring the outports, coves, and rivers of the area. The project for the winter of 1964 was to complete *Westviking*. Mowat had been developing his own theory of the Vikings' discovery and settlement of Labrador and Newfoundland based on his reading of their sagas, navigational charts, and ancient maps. In the spring there were visits to Boston, Toronto, and St. Pierre and Miquelon to make a film about the French islands for CBC Television, *Boy on Vacation*. He had already done some work on scripts for the CBC — *Explorations* (1959), *Portraits from the Sea* (1963), and *Boy on Vacation* (1963). Indeed, he was being invited for his commentary, readings, and film vignettes more and more over the years and was beginning to develop a public personality to go with his books — that of a somewhat eccentric rascal who could be counted on to go against the fashionable tide of establishment opinion, a jester who insisted on being the conscience (albeit from the subconscious) of the nation.

Meanwhile, all sorts of events were keeping Farley and Claire busy as they continued to explore the province. A friend who had a Beaver plane with pontoons flew them into the abandoned settlement of La Hune where they observed six fin whales offshore. Because four fin whales spent each winter near Burgeo, they had developed a particular interest in these creatures. The Mowats also studied the sea-life during their trip to outports that July. Claire reports that on one trip they amused themselves for a few evenings by reading Jerome K. Jerome's *Three Men in a Boat*, which she found so funny that she suggested to Farley that he consider writing a book about *Happy Adventure*, a suggestion he fortunately took to heart by writing *The Boat Who Wouldn't Float*. The mail brought more journals and diaries of explorers for another edition in what would become a series on arctic travellers. That fall of 1964, Farley persevered with the final draft of *Westviking*, while Claire drew the maps for the book. Fortunately, the weather was bad enough to keep away distractions until it was finished.

At this time Farley also became involved in getting a bridge built for the people of a small nearby island, a cause that led to his meeting the provincial premier, Joey Smallwood, with whom Mowat developed a cordial relationship. Claire began to teach an art class at the local school, while Farley helped to solicit books for the library and started to put together notes for another story for young people called *The Curse of the Viking Grave*. The only sour note that year was the news that Angus had decided to leave Helen for a thirty-nine-year-old librarian with whom he had fallen in love. He left Port Hope and moved into a cabin he built north of Kingston. From this time on, the relationship between father and son remained strained. Angus was still expecting a "serious" novel from his son instead of the kinds of things he had produced so far.

A Whale of a Celebrity

The family crisis necessitated numerous trips to Ontario the following year, though Mowat also went to Boston to revise *Westviking* at the home of Peter Davison. As usual, the book

A portrait photo for McClelland and Stewart, c. 1978

came out that fall. A trip to Mexico and the United States with Harold Horwood took up most of the winter and settled outstanding legal details concerning his divorce so that Farley and Claire could be married that spring of 1965. The summer he spent on his boat working on the two books he had started the previous fall. One of these, *The Curse of the Viking Grave*, a sequel to *Lost in the Barrens*, is a sort of travelogue for young adults describing the territory around Nueltin Lake. The story of Jamie, Awasin, and Peetyuk, introduced in the first book, picks up the next summer when the boys return to the Viking grave to retrieve and sell the relics in order to earn enough money to save Uncle Angus and the starving Inuit. They are joined by Awasin's sister, Angeline, who not only attracts Peetyuk but saves the boys on two occasions. Mowat did not much care for the book, possibly because it sags badly in the middle, but it does make his point that people from the south had disturbed the equilibrium of an ancient people's lives without considering the consequences. The three traditional enemies — whites, Cree, and Inuit — are represented here by the young people who, though they have their quarrels, learn to respect the differences among them and help each other to survive.

Mowat wrote from May to the end of August before he was off again on behalf of his publisher. An extensive publicity trip across Canada and back again for *Westviking* was tiring. In fact, for the next two years, the many distractions meant that his writing was of a rather scattered variety. He wrote articles for magazines, edited more exploration pieces for *The Polar Passion*, the second volume in his arctic travellers series, and wrote scripts for the CBC on the north, on Newfoundland, and on ecological issues. In March of 1966 he was flown by helicopter to St. John's for a dinner in his honour given by Joey Smallwood in recognition of Mowat's writings about the province. The columnist Jack Batten tells a story of another party thrown by Jack McClelland around this time at which Mowat noticed that the woman Batten had escorted had removed her half-slip because it refused to stay up. In a sympathetic gesture Mowat, who often wore a kilt to these affairs, took off his underpants and threw them away. In an interview two years later, quoted by Batten, Mowat acknowledged he did this every once in a while to shock a complacent society:

"Well, initially it was a need to shock, to substantiate my own ego, to reinforce my own evaluation of myself. I don't need that any more, but I still do it because it's amusing, it's an entertainment, it's great fun to upset someone who's been living in a box all his life."

It was also good for book sales.

The year 1966 was hectic with travel. *Maclean's* flew Mowat to Spence Bay, in the Northwest Territories, to cover the trial of two men accused of killing a woman, apparently the mother of one of them, who had gone mad and presented a danger to the community. Mowat's article, later revised to become "The Dark Odyssey of Soosie" in *The Snow Walker*, emphasized that the woman's madness was the result of years of dislocation and confusion, largely a consequence of a policy designed to force the Inuit to conform to the laws of white society. Mowat also visited Yellowknife, Povungnituk, and a number of other northern settlements on this trip. Jack McClelland was impressed with Mowat's renewed enthusiasm for the north and agreed to a $10,000 advance for a book for the Canadian Illustrated Library series called *Canada North*. Mowat, gathering material for use in this book and for a series of programs for CBC Radio, flew to Churchill, chartered an Otter aircraft, and visited thirty-three additional settlements.

Ever since his books had been translated into Russian, Mowat had been in touch with several Soviet writers, one of whom, Yuri Rytkheu, a Chukchee or northeasterner, invited him for a visit. Curious to compare the northern settlements and policies of the two countries, Mowat made arrangements for a trip from Montreal to Leningrad aboard the ship *Alexander Pushkin*, completing *Canada North* along the way. He and Claire then visited Helsinki, Leningrad, and Moscow before being taken to the Siberian cities of Omsk, Irkutsk, Baikal, and Novosibirsk. They were the guests of the Writers' Union — a group that had enough political clout to arrange for the Mowats to travel to these places and be feasted in each one. Even the long waits at airports were turned into parties, and the alcohol that seemed to appear everywhere fortified them against the plunging October and November temperatures as they moved farther north. Mowat's kilt was a big hit with the people but not too practical for the weather. They were taken to visit state farms, cooperatives, universities for question-and-answer sessions, concerts, and ballets. They flew in small planes over rugged mountains all the way to Tchersky on the Kolyma River — the first foreigners to visit that area since the revolution. In fact, Claire was the first foreign woman the people in Tchersky had ever seen. From there, they were taken by helicopter to the tundra to see reindeer herds, and Mowat was given a scroll declaring him to be an "Honorary Breeder of Reindeer" — the suggestion was made that the Mowats take up breeding the animals in Canada. Mowat was even taken by truck to Chukotka, a place off-limits because it is so close to Alaska. Back in Montreal in December, he spent three weeks working on a series of programs for the CBC based on the tape recordings he had made that summer.

After such an experience, Mowat was determined to write a book on Siberia but realized it would necessitate another trip. In the meantime, he and Claire retreated to Burgeo for some peace and quiet. The January 1967 crossing of the Cabot Strait to Port-aux-Basques from North Sydney took twelve hours because of a bad storm — this was a portent of things to come. When Mowat greeted his old acquaintance Captain Penney, as he recalls in A Whale for the Killing, he was reminded of the reasons he had moved to Burgeo in the first place: to "escape from the increasingly mechanistic mainland world with its March Hare preoccupation with witless production for mindless consumption; its disruptive infatuation with change for its own sake; its idiot dedication to the bitch goddess, Progress." Burgeo now boasted thirty-nine cars and trucks, though the roads barely existed. The workers at the fish plant were still struggling to unionize, and the owner had become the mayor. (In 1971, the workers finally went on strike and he shut the plant down and left the place for good.) As the Mowats approached the outport village, they saw the whales that usually fed in nearby waters. Again, on his first trip by boat to the post office, Mowat saw a family of three fin whales, down from around thirty in 1964, close to Messers Cove where the herring often got trapped. On 20 January, a pregnant female fin whale got herself trapped when she followed the herring over the cove into Aldridges Pond. Five plant workers took it into their heads to go after the whale with rifles the next day. On the third day, while the Mowats were out for their Sunday walk trying to spot bald eagles, more than thirty residents were using the whale for target practice while a large crowd watched from the shore. It wasn't until Thursday that two fishermen told the Mowats what was going on at the pond.

When Mowat investigated, he knew almost immediately that he was committed to saving the whale. He asked the plant manager, now mayor of the community, to use his influence to get the people to leave the whale alone; he alerted the Federal Fisheries office which said they were not interested in mammals; he called Montreal for the advice of an expert on whales and received no response; eventually he even called Jack McClelland and told him of his frustration. The local RCMP constable did what he could to stop the tormenting of the whale but was able to accomplish little. When some of the people ran the whale aground, Mowat went into a wild tirade. Clearly, he had begun to lose his romantic notions of these genuine and simple people in harmony with nature, though even in the face of these atrocities Mowat's romanticism went deep and he tried to rationalize the people's behaviour. In *In Search of Farley Mowat*, he says that the young men shot at the whale because they had been contaminated by their experience working on the Great Lakes boats during the summers; in other words, he refused to let go of his romantic notion of the outport people and chose instead to blame their behaviour on the culture of central Canada. However, when by the following Monday things were no better, Mowat decided to get the media involved by calling the Canadian Press head office in Toronto. The CBC picked up the story, much to the resentment of many of the local people who then began to turn on Mowat as a traitor to their community. The more he pleaded with them, the more they taunted him. Joey Smallwood replied to Mowat's request for aid by offering $1,000 to feed the whale and officially naming Mowat the whale's keeper. Photographers arrived from the

Farley with his dogs at Brick Point, 1984.

Toronto Star and the CBC, but the whale would not eat and the weather made matters worse. The following week, Mowat saw that the bullet wounds and propeller cuts were now badly infected. He could not get antibiotics in time, and the whale died. The fallout from the community was enough to impress upon the Mowats that they could no longer live in Burgeo. For the rest of that winter, Mowat was joined by the photographer John de Visser who took photos of the south coast for a book they planned to do together on Newfoundland. By May 1967, however, the Mowats were prepared to leave.

Perhaps Mowat's continual moving was consistent with his romanticism. Claire says that Farley seemed to fall in love with places but would then decide to leave them after awhile. In any case, they flew to Toronto and drove to Port Hope — partly because they could think of no place else to go — back to the area around Belleville and Trenton that Mowat had known as a child. His mother was in Port Hope and that was about as close as they themselves wanted to get to big-city life. They bought an old house at 25 John Street, rented the house in Burgeo for the next two years before selling it, and decided to sail *Happy Adventure* to Montreal just in time for the closing of Expo '67, Canada's Centennial World's Fair. After a good deal of struggle with the boat, they departed in August and limped into Montreal in September. At one of the official receptions they attended, they met Alexandra Yakovlevna Ovchinnikova, Chairman of the Yakut Autonomous Soviet Socialist Republic, with whom Mowat struck up plans for another visit to Siberia. In October they sailed back to Port Hope where the winter ice nearly finished off *Happy Adventure*. It had to be hauled up in Deseronto that spring, where it stayed for quite some time.

Consolidating Interests

Life in Port Hope became hectic very quickly. The Mowats were visited by their Chukchee writer friend, and Farley was bombarded with invitations to appear on radio and television programs. He also had to make the usual publicity rounds for

Canada North and *The Polar Passion,* and was recognized for his contribution to Canadian culture in the form of the Canadian Centennial Medal presented to him that fall. Since Mowat planned to go back to the Soviet Union with John de Visser, he had to apply for a visa. One of his favourite stories is about accepting the invitation to dine at the Ottawa residence of the Soviet ambassador with Angus and Claire. When it was mentioned that the RCMP always kept an eye on the embassy, Angus and Farley, as Mowat tells it in *My Discovery of America,* paraded on the roof making bagpipe noises, while the two Soviets, dressed in the Mowats' kilts, thumbed their noses at the presumed hidden cameras. The image of the recent winner of the Centennial Medal making mocking gestures at the symbol of Canadian peace, order, and good government speaks volumes about Mowat and his place in the contradictions that are an essential part of Canadian culture.

Anti-authoritarian, intensely nationalistic, environmentally aware, and passionately romantic, Mowat often found it difficult to control his language. An article in the *Ottawa Citizen* in March 1968, for example, reported that Mowat had declined an invitation to command the Colonel J. Sutherland Brown Volunteer Brigade, whose purpose it would be to defend Canada against an invasion by the United States. American Strategic Air Command bombers were apparently carrying out simulated attacks at the five-hundred-foot level over the Saskatchewan prairie. The article mentioned Mowat's claim that he had fired his .22 rifle at SAC planes flying over his backyard in Newfoundland in 1958, and related his suggestion that the brigade should send up red weather balloons in the flight paths. Again, this item did not go unnoticed by the security services in the United States. Although the whole article was filled with irony and hyperbole (a .22 bullet could not come close to planes five miles above Newfoundland), it would rebound on Mowat later.

Around this time, the annual seal hunt began to attract public attention and Mowat took a growing interest in the problem. In February 1968, he observed seal herds from a light plane; the next month he flew by helicopter with de Visser and Brian Davies to the Magdalen Islands to witness the hunt there. While de Visser took pictures, Mowat interviewed sealers. He reported that he saw seal pups returning to consciousness while being skinned alive; he even remonstrated another man for killing an adult female that was trying to save her pup. Mowat concluded in *Sea of Slaughter* that the hunt itself was "an almost uncontrolled orgy of destruction conducted by, and for, people who were prepared to commit or to countenance almost any degree of savagery in order to maintain a high rate of profitability." In April he joined Canadian government scientists aboard the Norwegian sealer m/v *Brandal* to collect samples from the moulting patch of harp seals. Mowat says that the hunters recovered one of every five seals they shot. Off the sealing grounds of Labrador, he saw the great harp seal herd, about 250,000 seals on ice floes — a sight that made him that much more eager to stop the massacre.

After Farley and Claire journeyed with David Blackwood to the northern bays of Newfoundland, Mowat returned to Ontario and began work on a CBC Television film called *Voyage to the Sea of Ice*, the story of one of the last of the big schooners, which was aired the next March and October before being sold to the BBC. When the quiet of summer arrived, they moved into a little cottage on Lake Ontario where Farley tried to write a book on the aboriginal water dogs of Newfoundland, a project he abandoned after a couple of months. His book on Newfoundland with John de Visser, *This Rock within the Sea*, was published in the fall, and the Mowats welcomed a mate for their dog Albert — a Labrador puppy they called Victoria. The year ended with a brief vacation to Jamaica where Mowat toyed with the idea of a book on the underwater life of coral reefs.

Clearly, Mowat's writing had lacked firm direction for the last little while, though in the winter of 1969, he took up Claire's idea of a humorous book about *Happy Adventure*. Meanwhile, they both missed the ocean, so that spring they explored Nova Scotia, Cape Breton, and the Magdalen Islands looking for a place to buy. Most of June and July was spent in the Magdalens making a film for the CBC. They had rented a place in Breton Cove, Cape Breton, and that is where they spent the rest of the summer with Mowat's two sons and Dorothy Spencer, a good friend from Burgeo. The quiet hiatus was a boon considering the pace they would keep for the next four months.

The second journey to Siberia with John de Visser began in September. From Moscow they flew to the northeast, visiting such sites as an aluminum smelter at Shelekov, the shore of the Sea of Okhotsk, universities, and a leather plant at Yakutsk where Mowat met his old acquaintances, Nikolai Yakutsky, Simeon Danielov, and Moisie Efrimov. They were taken on a snowshoe rabbit hunt which Mowat joined for fun — he had given up killing animals after the war. What he learned was the way these Arctic peoples had adapted to the climate and the soil, how they had used new technology, but seemed to respect the ecology of the place, although some places such as Mirny were ugly and artificial to Mowat. Even Diamond Mine Number 3 did not impress him. The hydroelectric plant at Chernychevsky was a wonder, as was the hydrofoil ride to the outlying settlements of Zhataj and Pokrovskoe. Most of all, he liked the irrepressible people, especially the way many of them seemed suspicious of the technological and bureaucratic inroads being made in their land. As he wrote in *Sibir*, Mowat felt a kinship with their sense of being only one factor in the huge and complex equation of nature.

Their roots have not been severed. They remain a proud and integral part of the continuum of life.

It is not inconceivable that these enduring peoples may some day be the seeing-eyes to lead the rest of us (self-blinded by the glitter of our own Creation) into a better day.

If the people of Newfoundland turned out to be somewhat disappointing, the "Small People" of Siberia, with whom Mowat obviously felt empathy, now stood as the world's hope.

Mowat met Alexandra Yakovlevna Ovchinnikova, the dignitary he had met at Expo '67, who invited him to a celebration at which he drank fermented mare's milk, a very potent local ritual drink. Before leaving Siberia, he was once again taken to Tchersky and the camp of the reindeer herders where a 107-year-old shaman woman blessed him with the spirit of the deer — a gesture that moved him deeply. There were other equally impressive experiences: a visit to a burial mound at Zelyonny Mis (Green Cape); a visit to Cape Magadan where he was told shyly that his books were sold out at the local bookstore; a 55-kilometre trip over rugged mountains to Ola and its agricultural college; a stay at a spa in Talaya. There he seems to have been purged of all of the 100-proof Siberian hospitality, so he could be sent home in mid-November to begin a round of talks on Canadian radio and television publicizing *The Boat Who Wouldn't Float* which had recently been published. The tour ended on 22 December, just in time for Mowat to be home for Christmas.

The Boat Who Wouldn't Float was an instant success. The central metaphor is, of course, that of the frustrated narrator fighting a machine that refuses to do what it is supposed to do, thereby frequently putting the man in peril. The sea is the ever-present force in the background, ready to swallow up the man and his boat, if only to put an end to the farce. The Lorenzian/Luddite philosophy behind the anecdotes — Mowat was impressed by the writings of Konrad Lorenz — need not be taken too seriously, however, since the book is primarily a hilarious account of man's folly when he becomes the slave of his own inventions. The more confident and powerful a man is in this book, the more shocked and defeated he becomes by nature and by machinery. Only the local Newfoundlanders, who seem able to put the boat together (temporarily), have the proper perspective. The best example of the accommodation of the "natural folk" to technology is found in a scene worthy of Thomas Hardy describing his rustics. Jack McClelland plays the role of the overconfident city slicker, aghast at the behaviour of the locals:

Suddenly I heard Jack make a despairing, strangled sound. I spun around. . . .

All unaware of the scrutiny Enos was busy eating his bacon. It had proved too tough for him to deal with while his badly fitting dentures remained in his mouth, so he had removed both plates. He now held them firmly in the angle between thumb and forefinger of his left hand, and he was making them snap open and shut with a dexterity that argued long practice. With his right hand he was passing a strip of bacon between the two sets of grinders. When this remarkable operation had macerated the strip of bacon sufficiently he threw back his head, poised the bacon over his mouth, and gummed it down.

Jack struggled to his feet, pushed his way past me, and vanished out the companion hatch. Before he returned, an hour or so later, Enos had packed his gear and gone ashore. I cannot in all conscience say that either of us was deeply pained to sign him off.

Since most of the anecdotes are connected with the boat (sometimes a car) coming apart or flooding or stalling at the worst moments, only last-minute ingenuity of the Enos kind seems to save the day — and sometimes, their lives. The book won the Stephen Leacock Medal for Humour in 1970 (the rumour was that Mowat "mooned" the audience during his acceptance speech), and is still in print in many countries.

The medal for humour was not the only award Mowat received in 1970. He was also awarded an honorary doctorate in literature from Laurentian University in Sudbury, and the Canadian Authors' Association Vicky Metcalfe Award for his contribution to Canadian writing. The winter was spent writing about his trips to the Soviet Union, which resulted in a lively narrative published that fall, *Sibir*. Mowat's enthusiasm for the people drives the writing, although it is replete with the kind of hilarious anecdote that he was now known for. The general message of the book is that the Canadian north had been treated as a no-man's-land by the Canadian government which, up to that time, had all but ignored its potential and, more significantly, its people. The United States security services made note of the book along with Mowat's public statements, beginning with an interview published in *Authors Take Sides on Vietnam* in 1967, protesting American military activities in Vietnam. Mowat got involved in more controversy that summer. He and Claire had bought a house on the northeast tip of the Magdalen Islands chain at Grande Entrée that year. When an oil spill from an Irving tanker covered hundreds of miles of the Magdalens' beaches with heavy oil, Mowat argued long and hard before they agreed to clean it up. That summer, too, the CBC made a documentary about Mowat's life in the Magdalens called "Me

An Aislin cartoon in the Toronto Star
commemorating Farley's 70th birthday in 1991.

and Albert"; it was aired on the program *Telescope* on 15 December 1970. In October, *Sibir* was published, which meant yet another cross-country tour.

The winter months of 1971 found Mowat occupied with a book on the seals and sealers of the North Atlantic, *Wake of the Great Sealers*. Mowat had also agreed to work on a film about Newfoundland with Max Braithwaite. In March, from his base in the Magdalen Islands, Mowat took an opportunity to witness the seal hunt. That summer, he and Claire entertained many visitors, including Pierre and Margaret Trudeau. She asked for one of Vicky's pups, soon to arrive, for her expected baby, and the Mowats sent her one that fall. The Trudeaus duly named the dog Farley. Meanwhile, the human Farley began yet another project — a book about the whale, "Moby Joe," that had been killed so recklessly in Burgeo four years earlier. The book, *A Whale for the Killing*, was nearly completed that winter, along with the third of the exploration writings for *The Top of the World Trilogy*.

Mowat also put together a script for a National Film Board film about his father, which was produced in 1971. The film, simply called *Angus*, presents his father in the winter of his life, dreaming of the sea while repairing his boat and singing folksongs of youthful desire. Underneath its rather sentimental, nostalgic text, the film is a tribute to Angus as the last of a type of rugged, romantic individualists. A trip to Scotland and then to Rome to visit with his editor, Peter Davison, in April of 1972 proved to be a pleasant diversion for Farley and Claire — there was even a stop in Paris for an international publishers' meeting. Davison had been a major influence in Mowat's career, shaping his work and encouraging his interests over a long period of time.

The Distraction of Politics

Over the next few years, Mowat's political activism intensified. He became president of a project to save the whales called Project Jonah, a fitting cause since *A Whale for the Killing* had just come out in the fall of 1972. He investigated stories of a raid on the breeding grounds of the double-crested cormorants of the Magdalen Islands which, some argued, were consuming the fish stocks in the area. The winter was spent writing the text for *Wake of the Great Sealers*. Mowat also received honorary doctorates from both the University of Lethbridge and the University of Toronto.

In the spring of 1973, Mowat heard of the plan of a tourist lodge operator in Churchill, Manitoba, to make money by setting up expeditions to hunt beluga whales in Hudson Bay. On his way to Lethbridge to receive his honorary degree, Mowat stopped in Winnipeg to discuss the situation with then premier, Ed Schreyer. When Schreyer heard of the scheme, he stopped it cold. The lodge operator was encouraged to take tourists out to see the whales along with biology students, who would be hired to explain the habits of the whales to them. This was the beginning of a close friendship between the Mowats and the Schreyers. Mowat had previously met with Jack Davis, then fisheries and environment minister, who had agreed to see if he could put an end to commercial whaling, the result of which was a ban on the hunting of large whales in the Atlantic region.

Political matters seemed to keep Mowat preoccupied for the next few years so that he wrote very little. He was active in promulgating the idea of a writers' union, for example, when the Royal Commission on Publishing met in 1973–74. He also kept busy organizing his papers which he had given to McMaster University in 1974, and there was the constant demand for interviews and articles on all sorts of topics. Mowat had by now made a number of friends in Canadian literary circles, including Marian Engel, who visited the Mowats in a house they rented on Cape Breton Island during the summer of 1975. That spring, Mowat and his son Sandy visited Scotland together. *The Snow Walker*, a collection of short stories, most of which had been published earlier, was issued in the fall, and involved another publicity tour. Meanwhile, the Mowats had moved out of their house in the Magdalen Islands in the summer of 1976 because of increasing tourism and the resultant growing resentment towards the English on the part of the French Canadians who lived there. In the fall of 1976, they bought Helen Mowat's house at 18 King Street, Port Hope, and moved in. That summer they also purchased a farm at Brick Point on Cape Breton Island where, from 1977 to the present day, they continue to spend each summer and fall.

An updated version of *Canada North*, complete with impressive photographs and retitled *Canada North Now: The Great Betrayal*, appeared in the fall of 1976. Its thesis was that things had not become any better for the Native peoples of the north in the ten years since Mowat's last report; if anything, they were worse. The culprits are the same: a blind government bureaucracy at every level; greedy corporations based mainly in the United States; a smug, indifferent population in southern Canada that treats the north as its colony. The impassioned plea was a familiar one: "If we have any survival sense at all, we will put an end to the Great Northern Giveaway and bring a halt to the despoliation of the northern lands and waters, and to the degradation of the northern peoples."

The first critical study of Mowat's writing appeared in 1976: a short monograph by Alex Lucas, published in McClelland and Stewart's Canadian Writers Series. This marked an attempt to situate Mowat in the tradition of Canadian literature and to file an interim report on the ideas and values outlined in his writings. It is a thoughtful study but ultimately did not bring Mowat's work to the attention of the academy. Perhaps not enough attention was paid to his lucid style or experimentation with form. At any rate, it acknowledged Mowat's stature as a significant Canadian writer. The fact that the academic community was slow to recognize the importance of Mowat's work could be the result of academics' justifiable distrust of popular writers, or the usual "peer sneer" (an unfortunate if inevitable product of the university system). However, Mowat's importance had already been established, if indirectly, by the cartoonists who loved to draw caricatures of Mowat as a Puck figure in the wilderness, or as a Scot smoking rum in his clay pipe. There is a veritable gallery of good-natured political cartoons featuring Mowat, by such cartoonists as Mosher (Aislin), Macpherson, and Franklin.

The following year was not a pleasant one. Although he was invited, in the spring, to visit Bulgaria as a guest of the Bulgarian

Writers' Union and the trip was a pleasant one, Angus's death in September of 1977 was a sad loss, and many matters had to be taken care of, which meant flying back and forth between Cape Breton and Ontario. In *In Search of Farley Mowat*, Farley says that when his father died he "felt a sense of liberation, a sense of freedom which was at odds with [his] sense of obligation, [his] memories of his father." In many ways his father's presence had been a weight for Farley that was lifted when Angus died. Now Farley was free to pursue his own form of writing without the guilt that had been instilled by Angus's disapproval of "popular" writing. It was just after this that Farley began to let go of what he calls, in *In Search of Farley Mowat*, the "false Mowats," including the clown, the heavy drinker, the iconoclast, and the TV Mowat, which no longer served their purposes.

Nevertheless, the loss of his father did take its toll, and both Farley and Claire became sick for a time. One bright spot was the news that he had won the Curran Award in Canada for his contribution to the understanding of wolves. The death of his father, however, seemed to release Mowat to write of his deepest feelings about his own war experiences and about war in general. During the winter of 1978, he started to write what is possibly his most enduring book, *And No Birds Sang*.

Mowat had actually decided to write a rather lighthearted book about the idiocies of military bureaucracy — his usual bête noire — but the book itself took over, and the winter was spent reliving the terrible years of his coming-of-age in Europe. There are signs of his initial plan at the beginning of the book: anecdotes about his enlistment, the way he lost his virginity and caught a venereal disease in the bargain, high jinks on training missions. When the invasion of Sicily begins, however, the story turns grim and terrifying. One of the controlling symbols in the narrative is that of a narrator who tries to keep watch of the birds: when he sees only birds of carrion, he is in the blackest part of the experience of war. Other motifs that knit the story together include the arbitrary behaviour of machinery, the enslavement of humans by their machines, the wanton destruction of nature for no good reason whatsoever, and the horror that can result from the casual incompetence of those in command. At the same time, there are descriptions of extraordinary acts of heroism, appalling tragedy, and courageous suffering and generosity. Throughout, the prose is well coordinated with the story's pacing and shifting tones. The book will no doubt go down as one of the finest pieces of writing on the Canadian effort in the Second World War that we have. It is also an effective plea against war in any form, at any time. It is perhaps significant that it is dedicated not to Angus, but to Mowat's mother, and to his wife.

Ladies in Waiting

In the spring of 1978, following the writing of *And No Birds Sang*, the Mowats travelled to Scotland and Iceland. The summer was spent as usual in Cape Breton at Brick Point. Mowat was awarded the Queen Elizabeth II Jubilee Medal, and that December he and Claire learned that their friend Ed Schreyer had been named the new governor general of Canada — the youngest man, at the age of forty-two, to be so named. In January of 1979, they attended his installation ceremony and visited the Schreyers often in Rideau Hall in the next years. Since the Mowats were so skilled at making people feel at home, something that seems to come naturally to them, they were frequently asked to Government House to help put strangers at their ease.

Mowat spent part of 1979 lobbying on behalf of the seals and whales, but seemed to get nowhere. The most unexpected event of the year was the return of *Happy Adventure*. It seems that it had been bought in Owen Sound by a sailor who had worked on the boats of the Great Lakes. He had somehow sailed the boat to Nova Scotia, must have heard that Mowat was in the province, and got it as far as Cape Breton, where Mowat bought the boat for the same price he had sold it, though really it was barely safe. When it was hopeless to think it could float any more, he ran it ashore and donated it to a local museum where it sat on the front lawn for a couple of years. Eventually, when the town could no longer afford to keep it, some friends offered to haul the boat to Margaree Harbour on a trailer, but along the way it apparently hit a bump in the road and fell to pieces, though the boat was later repaired. The year was capped with the publication, to very favourable reviews, of *And No Birds Sang*.

The National Film Board of Canada had been putting together a biography of Mowat called *In Search of Farley Mowat* which was released in 1981 (the video and shorter version for schools came out in 1983). Mowat's cousin, Andy Thomson, the producer of the film, persuaded Mowat to spend a great deal of time with him in 1980 working on the project. The film contains good interviews and photos, but rests on the premise that Mowat is an elusive personality whom one cannot "really" know.

Along with a number of such film projects, the 1980s were a time of travel for Mowat. The most interesting trip was hatched in January 1981, when the Mowats were visiting the Schreyers at Rideau Hall. The governor general had been invited on a state tour of the Nordic countries, the first such goodwill tour for a Canadian governor general. Lily Schreyer was expected to take along a lady in waiting, and she invited Claire to take on the responsibilities. Protocol had no role for Farley, however, so he was designated cultural advisor and was thus able to join the party. Claire wrote about the tour in a book entitled *Pomp and Circumstances*, an engaging description of the education of innocent civilians in the elaborate formalities of the diplomatic service. According to Claire, Farley had to buy the first three-piece suit he ever owned. He did not even have a two-piece suit since he had worn sweaters, slacks, and tweed or corduroy jackets all his life. His only formal wear had been his Scots regalia: kilt, velvet jacket, sporran, and shoes with silver buckles. The winter, in preparation for the tour, was spent shopping and learning formal rules of etiquette.

In February 1981, the ABC network aired a television movie version of *A Whale for the Killing*, and Robin Mathews published his stage adaptation of *The Curse of the Viking Grave* which had been first produced in 1980. There were similar ventures throughout the late 1970s and '80s. The BBC aired a four-part series on *Never Cry Wolf* in 1972, and the CBC program, *Take*

30, had run a two-part documentary on the Mowats in the Magdalen Islands in 1974. Czechoslovakia Radio broadcast a program called "Death of a Whale" the next year, and a radio station in Iceland broadcast a serialization of *Canada North Now* in 1978. In addition, there was a one-hour documentary called *The Polar People* on CBC's *This Land* in May 1978, a reading of *The Dog Who Wouldn't Be* for the BBC, and readings of Mowat's books for the radio networks of many other countries in that year and the years following. Mowat had control over only those projects in which he was directly involved; in some cases, he simply sold the rights and the final product was out of his hands. The results, such as the ABC production of *A Whale for the Killing*, were sometimes less than felicitous. Another such project was the film version of *Never Cry Wolf*, originally sold for $20,000 to independent producers which, when it got into financial trouble, was underwritten by the Disney Corporation which then controlled its release and advertising. The filming of the story faltered for a couple of years before the final cut was released in 1983 to a gala fanfare in Toronto attended by the Mowats, the director, Carroll Ballard, Jack McClelland, and the Schreyers. During the shooting, the producers had asked Mowat to visit the set near Whitehorse to boost the morale of the players and crew. When he arrived, he was offered a cameo role as a bartender who had to say a simple line and gulp some beer. After more than twenty-five takes, he was too tipsy to get the name "Rosie Lee" straight, confusing it with "Gypsy Rose Lee," until by the end it was all just foul language and they cut the scene completely.

There were similar amusing episodes during the Nordic tour with the Schreyers in May and June of 1981. The group landed in West Germany, and after the arrival of the external affairs minister, Mark McGuigan, they all set out for Stockholm, where the Mowats met the Swedish King and Queen and found themselves suddenly enmeshed in a bewildering labyrinth of protocol. In her book, Claire recounts their cheerfully accompanying the Schreyers to meetings with monarchs and dignitaries, until she and Farley learned that they were not supposed to be in attendance at all. No harm was done, but the blushing and giggling that seems to have followed many of these events set the tone of the trip. Added to these incongruities was the fact that Farley, because Claire was susceptible to motion sickness in small aircraft, sometimes acted as stand-in lady in waiting.

From Sweden, the group travelled by ship to Helsinki, Finland, where Mowat was enough of a celebrity that they demanded he agree to be interviewed on television. On the way out of Finland, there was some excitement when their Finnish ship hit a huge rock which an iceberg had moved into place during the spring thaw, cutting a gash in the ship's hull for about a third of its length and causing over a million dollars in damage. Next, they flew to Lapland over the Arctic Circle and visited a number of small cities and factory towns, then on to Norway, where, because Farley became a favourite of the King, they stayed in luxurious quarters, feasting with the country's dignitaries. From Norway they went to Denmark aboard the Canadian ship *Huron*, visiting small towns before meeting Prince Henrik and Queen Margrethe. The Mowats stayed in the King Christian Suite in the Royal Palace — an ironic place for Farley to find himself after a lifetime of healthy cynicism about the rich and pretentious. After a final foray into Iceland, they found themselves back in Ottawa, only to learn that Mowat was to be named Officer of the Order of Canada.

Mowat's writing career was recognized, in September 1981, by the release of the NFB/CBC biography, *In Search of Farley Mowat*. The film's director, Andy Thomson, deciding to leave the National Film Board, persuaded Farley to form a film company with him in order to make six half-hour films on the north — the "Polar Film Project" was its working title. They began with a trip to Greenland. Mowat says this film company, later called Norwolf/Noralpha, became a major disaster, but they did eventually produce a two-hour documentary on the polar region for CTV called *The New North*, aired in April 1989. In that year, 1982, Mowat received yet another honorary doctorate, this time from the University of Victoria, British Columbia. He also began work on a project he had considered for some time but had been reluctant to take on because it was such an enormous task — a history of the animals along the eastern seaboard. For the following two years he worked on *Sea of Slaughter*, while Claire wrote and published her fictional memoir of their time in Burgeo, *The Outport People*. Three times during the writing of the book, Mowat threatened to quit because the task was too big: the frequent use of statistics worried him; he could not seem to keep his emotional reactions in check; he was reluctant to limit himself to the eastern seaboard when he had more evidence of the extinction of the wolves and bears in the northwest. Finally, shocked at the extent of the destruction, Mowat, in a rage, decided to forge ahead. The exercise gave him new admiration for environmentalists, of whom he had formerly been sceptical, and he began to support them wholeheartedly. He even decided that zoos were a terrible idea. Mowat saw his project to be akin to Rachel Carson's ominous 1962 bestseller *Silent Spring* in that it would establish a written record that conservationists could use. The promotional tour of *Sea of Slaughter* in the United States led to yet more controversy, the kind that got Mowat's creative juices flowing. Altogether, the book increased Mowat's involvement in the environmental movement over the next few years.

The year had been a productive one for Mowat, but it had also brought sadness, for Helen Mowat died in 1984. She had been a quiet and effective support for her son throughout his life. Because Mowat's father had been the dominant presence, Farley had grown inevitably into "a man's man," valuing and taking joy in typically male passions. His mother does not figure in the foreground of his writings, and in his children's books the mother is often left out altogether. Mowat acknowledged that he did not pay enough attention to his mother in his written work, but he realized that in many ways this was inevitable. She was a background force: taken for granted, but essential for all that.

Discovering America

By spring 1985, Ed Schreyer was Canadian high commissioner to Australia, and was visited there by Mowat who attended a writers' conference and lectured at some Australian universities under the aegis of Canada's External Affairs Department. Mowat had to return home in April in order to prepare for a trip to California at the invitation of Michael Bauman, a professor of English at California State University at Chico, just north of Sacramento. Mowat was supposed to discuss his work with the students there, while at the same time promoting his book on animal preservation along the East Coast as arranged for by the External Affairs Department. By late March, however, Bauman informed him that External Affairs had cancelled their commitment quite mysteriously, but that the publishers would take up some of the sponsorship. On 23 April, Mowat left Port Hope and arrived at Toronto's Pearson Airport, only to be stopped by United States Immigration; his luggage went through but he was not allowed into the United States. He contacted Jack McClelland, expressed the proper outrage, and the two went to McClelland's house in Kleinberg to find out what had happened. They contacted Peter Davison in Boston who confirmed that the Justice Department was refusing Mowat entry, but that they declined to say why.

Characteristically, McClelland decided to fight back by alerting all the media in Canada, while Davison did the same in the United States. Mowat thought that he was being kept out of the United States because of his trips to Siberia in the late 1960s, while McClelland speculated that the American gun and hunting lobby did not want the author of *Sea of Slaughter* in their country. Eventually, Davison found out that Mowat was being barred by the McCarran-Walter Act, which excludes anyone from entering the country who is suspected of being an enemy — especially a Communist. Mowat was told by American officials that they had a file on him, and that if he met them at the border, they would go over it with him. He declined their patronizing attitude. Perhaps it was his sponsorship of the Fair Play for Cuba Committee in the early 1960s, he thought, or maybe his association with the Campaign for Nuclear Disarmament, his anti-Vietnam War activism, or all the other anti-war groups he had publicly supported that had created this bizarre situation. But then it could also have been his support of the Coalition Against Acid Rain or his involvement in Project Jonah.

On 24 April, and for the following week, Mowat joined with McClelland to counter the smear tactics by giving many radio, television, and press interviews. Eventually, Joe Clark, then minister of external affairs, got in touch with Mowat to say he would contact the American immigration authorities; Clark never called back. Mowat, meanwhile, was demanding a public apology from Ronald Reagan, then president, and a free trip to California aboard Air Force One. Prime Minister Mulroney called in his commiserations but did not seem to know what the problem was. Finally, a *New York Times* reporter told Mowat that his file recorded that he had threatened to shoot down United States Air Force planes and that he had actually taken a shot at a bomber at one time. Apparently the FBI had acquired a copy of the old *Ottawa Citizen* story of 22 March 1968. Malcolm Browne printed the current story in the *New York Times*, complete with the tongue-in-cheek tone of the original episode.

Mowat decided to return to Port Hope to rest, though he continued to be disturbed by innumerable calls, as well as an early morning interview on the NBC *Today Show*. By the end of the week, he read a dispatch from Washington saying that he would be allowed to enter the United States on a temporary waiver pending an investigation, although it seemed that his name would remain on the blacklist. Mowat, in turn, demanded complete clearance or nothing. The bureaucrats, Mowat's favourite target, then started their usual verbal mastications, hinting that he could "enter," but he was not being "admitted," while Mowat gleefully kept notes. On Monday, he got official notice of his permission to enter the United States but wrote back for clarification of specifics. Gradually, Mowat grew to suspect that Canadian External Affairs had known that he was not going to be admitted and had backed out early because the government did not like the criticisms he had made of its environmental bills in *Sea of Slaughter*.

When the whole affair died down, the Mowats retreated to Cape Breton where Farley transformed his notes into a satire of bureaucracy in *My Discovery of America*, published in the fall of 1985. Two things were cleared up for him around this time. He received a copy of his file from the United States authorities and found that his involvement in the Fair Play for Cuba Committee was listed there, along with his support of the Student Union for Peace Action, his activism in nuclear disarmament and aid for Vietnam civilians, his trips to the USSR, and the Ottawa newspaper report that he had fired his .22 rifle at an American plane. The second thing Mowat discovered was that the American people had written many letters of support, and that the American press was very much on his side. He learned, therefore, that his long-held belief that the American people backed the policies of their administration was not an accurate assessment. In a letter to Michael Bauman printed in *My Discovery of America*, Mowat tells how he took heart "in the impassioned rejection by so many [Americans] of the authoritarian, undemocratic, and frequently underhanded procedures employed against all of us 'excludees' by those who are supposed to serve, and do your will."

In December 1985, in what seems like a further defiant gesture, a parting shot for the whole event, the Mowats accompanied Margaret Atwood and Graeme Gibson on a trip to Cuba to do some bird-watching. Mowat returned to find that he and his publisher were the targets of a legal suit launched by the Canadian Wildlife Federation over passages in *Sea of Slaughter*. They charged that Mowat had defamed them by insisting that they were inciting people to kill wolves. The suit became a nuisance to Mowat for the next two years before it was dropped, but not before it had cost him $30,000. The same amount in legal fees was picked up by McClelland and Stewart. Mowat felt that it was part of a scheme to get him to stop agitating for animals and the environment in the future.

Inveterate travellers by now, the Mowats went off to New Zealand for a month in February of 1986. In August and September, Farley took part in the filming of *The New North* in the Canadian Northwest, Scandanavia, and Siberia. A two-hour production, the film is narrated by Mowat and William Hutt and follows Farley on a journey to Siberia, Greenland, Sweden, and the Canadian far north. In this film one gets a clear sense of Mowat's ebullient personality, his passion for the proper development of the world's tundras, and his respect for the wisdom of the traditional ways the indigenous peoples have

legacies   many of
~~Such~~ wounds to minds and bodies ~~whichxtheyx~~ would isable t hem until they

reachedwhat w as all t oo often an early grave. ~~Apart xfromxthesexx~~

~~Canadaz hadxdonexzxexthexxwallx~~
                But
                Apart from these,~~Canadianzxhadzdonexxxxthexzwallx~~ "unfortunates"

                                        and Canadians
~~Canadiansxhadxindeedxdonexxthexxwallz~~ ~~Canada had~~ come out of the War

        making to walk Spr for Democracy, as my Father used to say, Spr for Plutocracy, ~~but~~
lapt Canada
        ~~(in~~ fine fettle. Trenton, and Ontario was a case in point.

                                                            about)
    In 1914 Trenton had been an overgrown village of ~~[~~a thousand

        mostly of English, Scots and Irish forestry,
~~or so~~ people ~~[~~grouped around a natural harbour at the mouth of the Trent

                Runs
River which ~~ran~~ down from the ~~forestxxxxxed~~ north country to empty

into the ~~placidxgratx well~~ protected waters of the Bay of Qunite. The

towns folk mostly took their livlihoof from trade with the farms which

stercthed northward from the bay shore for some twenty or thirty miles

                            the   once
until they scarbbled out in the hard rock,and pine forests, ~~which were the~~

                            During much of the 19th century
~~domain of timbermen and miners.~~ ~~Once upon a time~~ the timbermen had

        this interior   been)
been the kings of ~~the~~ region and great rafts of logs had ~~run down the~~

                to a cluster of belching lumbermills around Trenton harbour.
Trent every spring. But by 1914 the ~~timberzeadz~~ good timber was ~~mostlyz~~ lng

            remaining
gone and the only ~~[~~vestige of the days of the great rape of the forests

                    on the harbour shore)
was a sprawling cooperage mill ~~[~~producing hardwood barrels. Apa t from

            a few other such   the mill The Mill
a carriage works and some ~~tiehr~~ small scale manufactureries, ~~the MILL~~

    Trenton's   industrial
was ~~ribeton's~~ only notable ~~industry commercial~~ ~~industpyzz~~ enterprise ()

~~and industrial employer.~~ ~~Farmers,xmexzghentxxandxlabxexexx~~ and labpurers

Manuscript page from Mowat's autobiography, "Born Naked."

learned to adapt to their fragile environment. Mowat expresses enthusiasm at the idea of some sort of union, even if just to share information, of these unique ecological areas of the planet. This film, along with *Sea of Slaughter*, is one of the best examples of how Mowat used the television medium as an extension of his subjective nonfiction form. However, around this time there were negotiations with Atlantis Films to take over the film company, Norwolf, though Mowat later regretted getting involved in the whole scheme. That year he also picked up another honorary doctorate from Lakehead University in Thunder Bay, Ontario, and he was the subject of a video released by Mead Sound Filmstrips in its Meet the Author Series. All in all, there were many distractions to keep him from writing.

Kindred Spirits

Jack McClelland persuaded Mowat to get back to his writing by proposing that he work on a biography of Dian Fossey, a woman who had spent the best part of her life studying gorillas in the wilds of Rwanda, Africa. Mowat preferred writing about subjects that came from his own experience, so he was reluctant to take on the project. However, he had a good deal of help from an associate, Wade Rowland, who furnished Fossey's archives. Rowland also collected interviews from people who had known Fossey, so that Mowat, as he states in *Virunga*, found himself in the position of what he called "an editorial collaborator." In the process of writing, Mowat discovered a kindred spirit in Dian Fossey — particularly in her sense that the animals held some sort of transcendental value, connecting humans with the rest of nature. Mowat had felt similar things ever since he was young, feelings that had grown into a philosophy he had defended in every way he could. No doubt, he felt that Fossey's murder was somehow an inevitable tragedy, given his own experiences when he had pleaded on behalf of the Inuit, wolves, and whales of his own country. He saw Fossey as the conscience of contemporary American society, just as he had tried to fill that role in Canada; both, in this sense, were mavericks, insisting that society's assumptions were questionable and had to be thought over. Mowat felt that he, too, had acted as something of a social conscience for Canadians, but that he had been written off by the established powers as a loudmouth, a gadfly, an irrelevance. Yet his book sales had always been a reminder that a great many ordinary people wanted to hear from him. Fossey was one of those individuals who, he said in a 1987 interview for *Maclean's*, "possibly help lead us out of the prison we are building for ourselves — this human prison in which we become aliens on an alien planet."

That summer in Brick Point, Mowat fell from a ladder, damaging both feet and dislocating his elbow. This called for some rest, but he did manage to get out of Norwolf, the film company that had partially drained his physical and financial resources. Jack McClelland called to say that his publishing company was bankrupt and would have to be sold. Mowat, who had published most of his books with that company, spent $75,000 to buy a unit-and-a-half of the holding company that was set up to buy McClelland and Stewart. When *Virunga: The Passion of Dian Fossey* was published in October 1987, Mowat went on what he decided would be his last major promotional tour. These publicity junkets were becoming too time-consuming and exhausting. Subsequently, in 1988, *Virunga* was proclaimed Book of the Year by the Foundation for the Advancement of Canadian Letters, and Mowat was given the Author of the Year Award by the Canadian Booksellers Association. The success of the new book was celebrated with a trip to Fiji and Christmas in Australia with the Schreyers.

The next project was to be a book called "The Green Crusaders," a series of interviews and commentaries on the environmental movement in North America. Again, Mowat was to work with Wade Rowland, but coordination fell apart and only Mowat's interviews were published in a collection entitled *Rescue the Earth!*, a book which was reasonably well received but with which Mowat himself was not satisfied. (Wade Rowland's contribution was slated to be released separately as "Front Line" but was never published.) The book, published in 1990, is intended as a guide to patrons of the environmental movement who want to know what is being done with their money. Perhaps the most interesting aspect of the collection, however, is the way it outlines the separate and often conflicting objectives of the various environmental groups in North America, a muddle which continues to bother Mowat.

In 1989, Mowat received a Gemini Award for Best Documentary Script for *The New North*, finally telecast on CTV as a two-hour documentary on 9 April 1989, though he was a bit scornful of the award because the final cut of the film had only a little of his writing left in it. A more exciting event was the publication of Claire Mowat's account of their state tour with the Schreyers, *Pomp and Circumstances*. If it can be said that Farley Mowat's writing is in the well-established Canadian literary tradition of exploration, travel, adventure, and animal writing — the imaginative mapping of the country — then it is also true that Claire Mowat's books are in the oldest tradition of Canadian women writers who described their reactions to the frontier and to new places and cultures — Frances Brooke, Susanna Moodie, Catharine Parr Traill, Anna Brownell Jameson.

For the last few years, Farley Mowat has divided his time among various projects, many of which have interested him for a long while. He is still committed to the belief that the Europeans came to North America long before we think they did. In his "West Man Project," Mowat has been trying to amass the evidence for this theory, though he has picked up his investigation and put it down again a number of times recently. In 1988, he put together a collection of anecdotes and descriptions of Newfoundland which was published in 1989 as *The New Founde Land*. He also spent a good deal of time helping to write and narrate a film version of *Sea of Slaughter* for the CBC series *The Nature of Things*, a project that involved his travelling to various locations for the shooting of the film. The experience of viewing the film, which was televised as a two-hour documentary on 14 January 1990, is somewhat like visiting an abattoir or slaughterhouse, though that was the intended effect. *Sea of Slaughter* was subsequently shown at an ecological film festival in Bristol, England, where it won the Conservation Film of the Year Award; Mowat himself was given an Award of Excellence at the 1990 Atlantic Film Festival in Halifax for "outstanding achievement in narration," and the 1990 Canadian Achievers Award by Toshiba Canada. The film version of *Sea of Slaughter* has been shown around the world in the last few years and has gained recognition as an important work in the wildlife/ecological movement. Recently, Atlantis Films has produced television adaptations of *Lost in the Barrens* and *The Curse of the Viking Grave*, aired in 1990 and 1992 respectively. Although Mowat did not contribute to these films — they are very different from their sources — his reputation as a writer for children has been more widely recognized as a result.

When Mowat reached the age of seventy in May 1991, Seal Books organized a huge birthday celebration in Toronto in July. That year, he was also presented with the first Take Back the Nation Award by the Council of Canadians for his contribution to Canadian nationalism and environmentalism. The Aislin cartoon of Mowat that seemed to appear whenever he was in the news showed up again and, of course, traded on his reputation as a hard-drinking Scot. The press commentary surrounding the two events was as good-natured as ever. In response, Mowat released a serious message, published in *Leisure World*, which too few newspapers and magazines carried:

> We are behaving like yeasts in a brewer's vat, multiplying mindlessly while greedily consuming the substance of a finite world. If we continue to imitate the yeasts we will perish as they perish, having exhausted our resources and poisoned ourselves in the lethal brew of our own wastes.
> Unlike the yeasts, we have a choice. What will it be?

There can be no clearer capsule comment of Mowat's concerns.

He had intended to tour Greenland again in the summer of 1991, but the plans fell through, so with extra time on his hands, Mowat began to go through old papers with a view to writing an autobiography, something he had been planning on and off for years. He found, amongst other things, most of the letters he had exchanged with his parents during the war, and became so involved with these that he spent the summer and the next winter working them into a book that would give some indication of the kinds of tensions and relationships that existed between Canadians at home and those fighting in Europe. The letters also help fill in the war years from the time the narrative of *And No Birds Sang* stops, to the time Mowat received his honourable discharge from the army. The edition of letters, with bridges of commentary added here and there, was published as *My Father's Son* by Key Porter Books in the fall of 1992. In the same year, Claire published her first very lovely book for children, set in Newfoundland, entitled *The Girl from Away*.

The substance of the events of *My Father's Son* has been included in this portrait, but it is also evident from Mowat's book that he has reconciled any lingering disappointment he may have had in his father. The book is a recognition of his father's steady influence in his life and an acknowledgement of his debt to him. The exercise allowed Mowat, at the age of 70, working in his caravan in Cape Breton where he does his writing, to rediscover his father, this time from the perspective of maturity rather than youth. It made an enormous difference, of course. He also had an opportunity to take a closer look at the young man he had been during the terrible interlude the war had been in his life, a man he found to be almost a stranger — tolerable, naïve, embarrassing in his relationships with women, but a survivor and an optimist beneath the bravado and the fear and the rage. Most important of all was the recollection, almost a newly discovered insight, that his parents had so cared and supported him throughout the ordeal.

Reprise

There have been three major phases in Mowat's life as a writer and thinker. His earliest years established his sense of wonder and curiosity, especially in the realm of animals and the open hinterland, because he moved from place to place, had pets for friends, and was introduced by his father, uncle, and their friends to the rugged freedoms of untamed spaces. He also had the patient support of his mother, with her traditional social and religious values, as a secure emotional base. Mowat felt like an outsider, not only because he often had to fit into different social groups, nor only because of his size, but also because his interests were largely directed by his rather unconventional father. Making the necessary adjustments for social and emotional survival, he grew to cherish solitude when necessary; found refuge in nature, pets, and books; accepted an image of himself as different; and gradually learned to trade on his hard-won individuality with ironic self-deprecation that cut both ways. He learned the tactic of remaining stubborn in a bluff, and no doubt began to apply his quickness of mind and sense of humour to the development of keener social skills.

The second phase in Mowat's development was largely the result of his wartime experiences. He had enlisted mainly to impress his father and to live out the adventures of romantic heroes; he was certainly not alone in that. The horrors of war profoundly challenged his fledgling romanticism, but in response Mowat searched for its validation in remote areas — the Natives of the barrenlands, and the birds, animals, and fish that seemed to be just as vulnerable to extinction as the People of the Deer. The war had clarified for him who and what the enemy was: a malignant, unfeeling bureaucracy fed by the greed of capitalist enterprise, and a blind faith in industry and technology that often enslaves and kills everything in its way, including those who devised it in the first place. Mowat's vision was a moral and humanitarian one, the driving force behind his writing, and he was optimistic that reform was possible. He knew early on, however, that he could love only individuals; he had to rail at the masses. Thus, Mowat used every tool he found — satire, hyperbole, iconoclastic tirades, programs to educate Canadians about their historical traditions and values, documentaries dressed up with techniques of persuasion and rhetoric. If film and television became the most useful communication device, he took to them quickly.

The third phase developed naturally out of the second. Mowat's vision has remained resolutely uncomplicated. In numerous interviews he has insisted that if one tries to include all the details and ambiguities and statistical dynamics of an issue, one is in danger of losing sight of the central problem. That is why he has resisted a more rigorous academic approach and tried to steer away from statistical data and surveys or reports from corporate or government sources. His defence has been to insist that *history* exists in the mind of the teller; the *truth* is in the telling. When his data, his sources, or his memory have been challenged, Mowat has offered a romantic reply: that he relies on his "subconscious memory" which never lies. So what he writes, he insists, is "subjective non-fiction." He takes his facts, his experiences, his sources, and "soaks in the truth" that is gleaned from them. The subconscious mind will then provide an intuitive sense of the truth of the matter at hand. Mowat as writer communicates that truth as powerfully and engagingly as he can. That way he can write passionately about what he truly believes, undistracted by peripheral concerns, uninfluenced by outside self-interested parties. He has consistently avoided writing pure fiction, with the exception of three children's novels, because a completely invented set of actions and characters would not be connected nearly so intimately with his own subconscious feelings, folded, as they are, into his own experiences. The passion would be missing, and thus so would the "kick" for both writer and reader.

As Mowat gets older, and as his moral crusades seem to be gaining inches rather than miles, he has become, not unexpectedly, more pessimistic. He says the war taught him that modern man was mad and therefore doomed, and he has had no reason to change his opinion. Yet his books imply a different perspective, which suggests that Mowat's pessimistic predictions are really the defence of a disappointed reformer. More recently, he has pleaded for an end to the wanton slaughter of animals and for a quick implementation of population control measures. He sees the planetary equilibrium being thrown out of balance, a delicate and unintelligibly intricate structure being torn to pieces by a careless and selfish species — Homo sapiens. Increasingly, Mowat's rhetoric indicates that we are rapidly reaching the point of not being able to undo the damage. Sometimes he admits this may be just as well, since the planet would then be rid of its worst enemy. While he may still be posturing for effect in order to wake up Canadians, there are signs that his mood is as gloomy as it sounds. In the meantime, however, even if prophets must inevitably sound jeremiads as they enter old age, Mowat has lost neither his sense of humour nor his compassion. These are his graces, a gift for all those who heed him.

Chronology

1892   Angus Mowat is born to Robert and Mary Mowat in Trenton, Ontario.

1915   Angus joins the Fourth Infantry Battalion. He is wounded and sent home the next year.

1919   Angus marries Helen Thomson and they eventually settle in Trenton.

1921   Farley McGill Mowat is born in Belleville, Ontario.

1922   Angus becomes a librarian in Trenton, thus starting a lifelong career.

1928   The family moves from Trenton to Belleville.

1930   The family moves to Windsor.

1933   The family moves to Saskatoon in midsummer. For the next three years, Mowat roams the prairie studying the wildlife and collecting pets.

1935   Mowat accompanies his uncle, Frank Farley, to Churchill where he sees the caribou migration and meets the Native peoples.

1936   Mowat writes a column on birds for the *Saskatoon Star Phoenix* and puts out his own pamphlet on nature studies with a few friends.

1937   The family moves to Toronto; Mowat spends time at the Royal Ontario Museum while attending school.

1938   The family moves to Elgin Mills, Ontario, where Mowat attends Richmond Hill High School. He decides to become a professional biologist.

1939   In the summer, Mowat and some friends drive to Saskatchewan to study birds. The war breaks out.

1940   The family moves to Richmond Hill, Ontario. Mowat enlists in the Hastings and Prince Edward Regiment.

1941   Mowat spends the year in various army training camps as he moves into the officer ranks.

1942	He arrives in England in July to join his regiment.
1943	In June, he is part of the assault on Sicily. The fighting is intense for the next year as he and his platoon move with the regiment through Sicily to southern Italy and fight their way north to Ravenna.
1945	Mowat publishes war stories in *Maclean's*. He is stationed in Belgium and Holland and begins a project to collect German armaments to be shipped to Canada for study.
⫯1946	He receives his honourable discharge and goes to Saskatchewan to study birds. In the fall he enrolls at the University of Toronto.
1947	In the spring, he goes north into the barrenlands to study the people who live there. He spends the summer around Nueltin Lake as a field biologist for the Dominion Wildlife Service, ostensibly to study wolves, but becomes involved in the plight of the Ihalmiut people of the region. In December, Mowat and Frances Thornhill are married.
1948	After the university term ends, he returns to the Nueltin Lake area and spends time helping the starving people there and studying their culture. He begins to write about his experiences in the north.
1949	Mowat graduates with a BA, settles in Palgrave, Ontario, and decides to become a professional writer.
1950	He publishes stories in the *Saturday Evening Post* and other magazines, gets an American agent, and begins work on *People of the Deer*.
1952	*People of the Deer* is published, and Mowat meets Jack McClelland who becomes his mentor and close friend. He receives the University of Western Ontario President's Medal for the best short story of the year, "Lost in the Barrenlands." He is also commissioned to write the history of his regiment.
1953	He and Frances tour Europe in preparation for the book on the regiment. Mowat continues to write and publish stories and articles.

1954   His son, Robert (Sandy), is born. Mowat sails to Halifax with his father and is attracted to the Maritimes.

1955   *The Regiment* is published. Mowat accepts a commission to write about the salvage ships of the Foundation Company. He begins to be active in nationalist organizations. As usual, he writes during the winter months.

✗1956   *Lost in the Barrens* is published and subsequently wins awards for children's literature.

1957   *The Dog Who Wouldn't Be* is published. Mowat takes his first trip to Newfoundland and admires the place and its people. He meets Harold Horwood. David Peter Mowat is adopted by Farley and Frances.

1958   *Grey Seas Under* and *Coppermine Journey* are published. Mowat explores Newfoundland and revisits the north. He discovers that the situation of the Ihalmiut is getting worse and decides to write about them again.

1959   *The Desperate People* is published. Mowat separates from Frances, leaves Palgrave, and is at loose ends for a time.

1960   He and Jack McClelland buy a boat in Newfoundland and together sail it around the south shore. Mowat meets Claire Wheeler at St. Pierre. *Ordeal by Ice* is published.

1961   He publishes *The Serpent's Coil* and *Owls in the Family*. That summer he goes sailing in the Maritimes with his father. He spends the winter writing in England.

1962   He and Claire travel in Europe, and Mowat visits his ancestral county in Scotland. That summer, they cruise around in Newfoundland waters and settle in Burgeo. *The Black Joke* is published.

1963   He finishes *Never Cry Wolf* and researches a book on the early Viking explorers.

1965   *Westviking* is published. They tour Mexico and the

United States. Mowat marries Claire Wheeler.

1966   Mowat attends a state dinner in his honour given by Joey Smallwood, premier of Newfoundland, and begins to cultivate his status as a celebrity. He flies to Spence Bay to cover a trial for *Maclean's* and begins work on a book and various films about the north. *The Curse of the Viking Grave* is published. The Mowats travel to the Soviet Union, including Siberia.

1967   The killing of a whale at Burgeo results in Mowat's alienation from the community. He and Claire leave and settle in Port Hope, Ontario. *Canada North* and *The Polar Passion* are published.

1968   Mowat becomes involved in the seal-hunt disputes and works on a book on Newfoundland with photographer John de Visser. *This Rock within the Sea* is published in the fall. He and Claire travel to Jamaica.

1969   They scout the Magdalen Islands for a summer home and spend time in Cape Breton. Mowat and John de Visser visit Siberia.

1970   *Sibir* is published. Mowat receives an honorary degree from Laurentian University in Sudbury, the first of six such degrees. He also receives the Stephen Leacock Medal for Humour for *The Boat Who Wouldn't Float*.

1972   Mowat visits Rome with his editor at Atlantic Press, Peter Davison. *A Whale for the Killing* is published. Mowat is president of Project Jonah and meets Ed Schreyer. He writes and narrates a film on his father. He and Claire look for another summer home.

1973   Mowat receives honorary doctorates in law from the University of Toronto and University of Lethbridge.

1975   The Mowats visit Scotland. *The Snow Walker* is published.

1976   They buy a summer home at Brick Point on Cape Breton Island and move in the following year.

1977   Angus dies. Mowat receives the Curran Award for his contribution to animal preservation.

1978	The Mowats take a trip in the spring to England, Scotland, and Iceland. Mowat receives the Queen Elizabeth Jubilee Medal. The Schreyers move into Rideau Hall on Ed Schreyer's appointment as governor general.
1979	*And No Birds Sang* is published. Mowat receives an honorary doctorate from the University of Prince Edward Island.
1980	Some time is spent on the film *In Search of Farley Mowat*.
1981	The Mowats accompany the Schreyers on a tour of Nordic countries. Mowat is named Officer of the Order of Canada.
1982	Mowat receives an honorary doctorate from the University of Victoria. He begins work on *Sea of Slaughter*.
1983	Film version of *Never Cry Wolf* is released. Claire's first book, *The Outport People*, is published.
1984	Mowat's mother, Anne Helen Mowat, dies. *Sea of Slaughter* is published.
1985	The Mowats visit the Schreyers in Australia. Mowat is refused entry into the United States to promote his book and discovers he is on their blacklist. *My Discovery of America* is published.
1986	Mowat works on a film, *The New North*. He receives an honorary doctorate from Lakehead University.
1987	*Virunga* is published. The Mowats visit Fiji and Australia. Mowat gets out of his film company, Norwolf/Noralpha.
1988	Mowat is named Author of the Year. The filming of *Sea of Slaughter* begins.
1989	*The New Founde Land* is published in the fall. Mowat receives a Gemini Award for Best Documentary Script for *The New North*. Claire's book *Pomp and Circumstances* is published.
1990	*Rescue the Earth!* is published. Mowat receives

various awards for his work on the film version of *Sea of Slaughter*.

1991   There are public birthday celebrations. Mowat wins the first Take Back the Nation Award for his contribution to Canadian nationalism and the environment.

1992   *My Father's Son* is published.

Works Consulted

Authors Take Sides on Vietnam. Ed. Cecil Woolf and John Bagguley. London: Peter Owen, 1967. 83–84.

Batten, Jack. "The Quintessence of Farley Mowatism." *Saturday Night* July 1971: 15–17.

Carver, Jos. E. "Farley Mowat: An Author for All Ages." *British Columbia Library Quarterly* 32.4 (1969): 10–16.

Dunlap, Thomas R. *Saving America's Wildlife*. Princeton: Princeton UP, 1988.

In Search of Farley Mowat. Dir. Andy Thomson. National Film Board of Canada, 1981. Videocassette, 1983.

Knelman, Martin. "Farley on Parade." *Toronto Life* Dec. 1983: 60+.

Lucas, Alex. *Farley Mowat*. Canadian Writers Series 14. Toronto: McClelland, 1976.

MacLulich, T.D. "The Alien Role: Farley Mowat's Northern Pastorals." *Studies in Canadian Literature* 2 (1977): 227–38.

Martin, Betty. "The World of Farley Mowat." *Canadian Author and Bookman* 45.2 (1969): 1–3+.

Mathews, Robin, adapt. "Farley Mowat's *The Curse of the Viking Grave*." *Playmakers: Adventures in Canadian Drama*. Ed. T. Binnersley and J. Milner. Ottawa: Steel Rail, 1980. 31–62.

Meet the Author: Farley Mowat. Sound filmstrip. Mead Sound Filmstrips, 1986.

Mowat, Angus. *Carrying Place*. Toronto: Saunders, 1944.

——. *Then I'll Look Up*. Toronto: Saunders, 1938.

Mowat, Claire. *The Girl from Away*. Toronto: Key Porter, 1992.

——. *The Outport People*. Toronto: McClelland, 1983.

——. *Pomp and Circumstances*. Toronto: McClelland, 1989.

Mowat, Farley. *And No Birds Sang*. Toronto: McClelland, 1979.

——. *Angus*. Dir. Andy Thomson. Prod. William Canning. Narr. Farley Mowat. National Film Board, 1971.

——. "Assessing an Outcast." With Suzanne Sandor. *Maclean's* 26 Oct. 1987: 12b–12d.

——. "Atlantic Rescue." Script. National Film Board, release date unknown.

—— [pseud. Bunje]. "Battle Close-Up," *Maclean's* 15 Feb. 1945: 19+.

——. "Birds of the Season." *Star Phoenix* [Saskatoon] 14 Mar.–9 May 1936, supp. *Prairie Pals*: 1.

——. *The Black Joke*. Boston: Little, 1962.

——. *The Boat Who Wouldn't Float*. Toronto: McClelland, 1969.

——. *Canada North*. Toronto: McClelland, 1967.

——. *Canada North Now: The Great Betrayal*. Toronto: McClelland, 1976.

——. *Canada's Role in Vietnam*. Willowdale: Conference for Canada's Role in Vietnam, 1965.

——, ed. *Coppermine Journey*. Toronto: McClelland, 1958.

——. *The Curse of the Viking Grave*. Boston: Little, 1966.

——. "The Desperate People." *Saturday Evening Post* 29 July 1950: 31+.

——. *The Desperate People*. Boston: Little, 1959.

——. *The Desperate People*. Rev. ed. Toronto: McClelland, 1975.

——. *The Dog Who Wouldn't Be*. Boston: Little, 1957.

——. "The Executioners." *Maclean's* 2 July 1966: 7+.

——. "Farley Mowat." With Alan Twigg. *Strong Voices: Conversations with Fifty Canadian Authors*. Madeira Park, BC: Harbour, 1988. 208–14.

——. "Farley Mowat — Last of the Saga-Men." With Jay Myers. *Canadian Author and Bookman*. 52.4 (1977): 4–7.

——. "Fighting Memories Pale beside 'Eving a Drink' in Bremen." *Saturday Night* 25 Aug. 1945: 33.

——. *Grey Seas Under*. Boston: Little, 1958.

——. "How They Suffered in Amsterdam! But Still There Was Carchio." *Saturday Night* 1 Sept. 1945: 25.

——. "How To Be a Canadian Writer — and Survive." *Saturday Night* 16 May 1953: 22–23.

——. "Lost in the Barrenlands." *Saturday Evening Post* 27 Oct. 1951: 28+.

——. *Lost in the Barrens*. Boston: Little, 1956.

——. "Maclean's Interviews: Farley Mowat." With Alexander Ross. *Maclean's* Mar. 1968: 9+.

——. "Me and Albert." *Telescope*, CBC Television, 15 Dec. 1970.

——. "Mowat's Metamorphosis." With Joan Lister. *Impetus* Feb. 1973: 29–30.

——. *My Discovery of America*. Toronto: McClelland, 1985.

——. *My Father's Son: Memories of War and Peace*. Toronto: Key Porter, 1992.

———. *Never Cry Wolf*. Boston: Little, 1963.

———. *The New Founde Land*. Toronto: McClelland, 1989.

———. *The New North*. Dir. Andy Thomson. Narr. Farley Mowat and William Hutt. Norwolf/Noralpha-NFB, 1987.

———. "On Being Mowat." *Maclean's* Aug. 1971: 24+.

———, ed. *Ordeal by Ice*. Toronto: McClelland, 1960.

———. *Owls in the Family*. Boston: Little, 1961.

———. "People of the Barrens." Narr. Farley Mowat. CBC Radio. 26 Mar. 1950.

———. *People of the Deer*. Boston: Little, 1952.

———. Unpublished interview. With John Orange. 26 May 1992.

———, ed. *The Polar Passion: The Quest for the North Pole*. Toronto: McClelland, 1967.

———. "The Polar People." *This Land*, CBC Television. 28 May 1978.

———. "Politics Kill Seals, Don't They?" *Maclean's* 15 Mar. 1982: 10.

———. *The Regiment*. Toronto: McClelland, 1955.

———. *Rescue the Earth!: Conversations with the Green Crusaders*. Toronto: McClelland, 1990.

———. *Sea of Slaughter*. Toronto: McClelland, 1984.

———. *Sea of Slaughter*. Dir. and Prod. John Brett. Narr. Farley Mowat. *The Nature of Things*. CBC Television. 14 Jan. 1990.

———. *The Serpent's Coil*. Toronto: McClelland, 1961.

———. *Sibir*. Toronto: McClelland, 1970.

———. *The Snow Walker*. Toronto: McClelland, 1975.

———. *This Rock within the Sea: A Heritage Lost*. Illus. John de Visser. Toronto: McClelland, 1968.

———. *True North*. National Film Board, 1987.

———, ed. *Tundra: Selections from the Great Accounts of Arctic Land Voyages*. Toronto: McClelland, 1973. Vol. 3 of *The Top of the World Trilogy* [with *Ordeal by Ice* and *The Polar Passion*]. 3 vols.

———. "The Two Ordeals of Kikik." *Maclean's* 31 Jan. 1959: 12+.

———. *Virunga: The Passion of Dian Fossey*. Toronto: McClelland, 1987.

———. *Voyage to the Sea of Ice*. Dir. Terry Richardson. CBC Television. 29 Mar. 1969.

———. "The Way of One Writer: Farley Mowat." *Canadian Library Journal* Feb. 1975: 56–57.

———. *Wake of the Great Sealers*. Toronto: McClelland, 1973.

———. *A Whale for the Killing*. Boston: Little, 1972.

———. *Westviking: The Ancient Norse in Greenland and North America.*

Illus. Claire Wheeler. Boston: Little, 1965.

———. "Why Story-Teller Farley Mowat Abhors Facts: They Get in the Way of the Truth." With Wayne Grady. *Books in Canada* Oct. 1979: 32–33.

———. *The World of Farley Mowat: A Selection from His Works*. Ed. and introd. Peter Davison. Boston: Little, 1980.

———. "Yeast of Eden." Letter. *Leisure World* Aug. 1991: 6.

Pimlott, Douglas H. Rev. of *Never Cry Wolf*, by Farley Mowat. *Canadian Audubon* Jan.–Feb. 1964: 27.

Porsild, A.E. Rev. of *The People of the Deer*, by Farley Mowat. *Beaver: A Magazine of the North* June 1952: 47–49.

Young, Scott. "Storm Out of the Arctic." *Saturday Night* 18 Oct. 1952: 16+.

York, Lorraine M. *Introducing Farley Mowat's The Dog Who Wouldn't Be*. Canadian Fiction Studies 7. Toronto: ECW, 1990.

imprimerie gagné ltée

 PRINTED IN CANADA